Praise for *Everybody Writes*

"Where was this book when I first started writing? Too many people think writing is easy: just put your thoughts down. Nope. Writing is much more dynamic in a world where content is everything and everywhere. In *Everybody Writes*, Ann Handley does the impossible: she teaches you (and me) how to not only tell better stories, but how to get those stories to connect with an audience. As usual, Handley does what she does best: she overdelivers. If you create content, buy this. If you run a team that creates content, buy everyone a copy. This is one of those books that will always sit within arm's reach of anyone who must come up with ideas."

—Mitch Joel
President, Twist Image;
Author of *Six Pixels of Separation* and *CTRL ALT Delete*

"This book provides marketers from all functions with a deeper understanding of this new era of storytelling and content, and it empowers them to contribute as a creative."

—Tim Washer
Senior Marketing Manager, Cisco

"Many people talk about the need to create great content, and to tell better stories in order to win new business in this social and digital age. So after cowriting the definitive *Content Rules*, Ann Handley is back to help us all understand how to get it done. Ann shatters the myth that writing is only for trained journalists, and provides amazingly insightful tips on how everyone can tell great stories."

—Michael Brenner
Head of Strategy, Newscred

"Handley gets to the core of why most content doesn't work. More important, she offers real-world, pragmatic advice for fixing it. Everyone who creates content for the Web—text, audio, or video—should read this book."

—Sonia Simone
Chief Content Officer, Copyblogger Media

"In our newly connected world, who would have thought that writing skills would be critical to an individual's future success? *Everybody Writes* gives you all the tools you need to make writing a core part of your life (and it needs to be). Plus, Ann's stories are incredibly engaging, she makes complex themes simple to understand, and she's just one really nice person (if you needed another reason)."

—Joe Pulizzi
Founder, Content Marketing Institute;
Author of *Epic Content Marketing*

"Great content marketing can't happen without great writing. But way too many marketing teams settle for 'good enough.' In this terrific book, Ann Handley shows why that's a fatal mistake and how to avoid making it. A fun, fast read that makes you want to run to your keyboard and tap out a masterpiece. But it's not just for writers, it's for anyone who commissions, edits, or works with writers."

—Doug Kessler
Cofounder and Creative Director, Velocity UK

"*Everybody Writes* is your guide to creating content you can be proud of and that customers will love you for. No one is going to win the content game with average, that's why *Everybody Writes* is a must-have guide for anyone that creates content."

—Lee Odden
CEO, Top Rank Marketing;
Author of *Optimize*

"Writing is one of the most important skills in marketing today. We all nod along while secretly wondering, 'How DO we get better at writing?' *Everybody Writes* addresses this in an accessible way that no other book has. As always, Ann does this with equal parts humor and heart. You'll laugh as you learn."

—Nick Westergaard
Chief Brand Strategist, Brand Driven Digital

"Writing is not an easy task. Writing a book about writing is near impossible, but Ann has done it as only she can. Filled with valuable information, techniques, examples, and smiles—this is the book for anyone who wants their words to have more success."

—C. C. Chapman
Author and storyteller

"Throw the others away because this is the only guide you need to elevate your content to the level of awesomeness! With wisdom and an infective wittiness, Ann shows you how to take your writing from awkward or awful to electric or elegant. She's your favorite teacher, cracking you up while her tough love gets you to do the work to improve. Even though I've written 10 books, I still learned a great deal in these pages and now I'm eager to flex my newfound content creation muscles."

—David Meerman Scott
Best-selling author of *The New Rules of Marketing and PR*

"The alternate click-bait title of Ann's great new book could have been 73 Ways to Improve Your Writing and Conquer the World! . . . and it would have been an understatement. We're all publishers now, and the better writers connect, persuade, and win. Be one of them with this book."

—Brian Clark
Founder and CEO, Copyblogger Media

"All your shiny new channels, properties, and platforms are a waste of space without smart, useful content. Ann Handley's new book helps make every bit of content count—for your customers and your bottom line."

—Kristina Halvorson
President, Brain Traffic

"I just glanced at the table of contents and I'm already a better writer. Ann Handley might just single-handedly save the world from content mediocrity. Really, really ridiculously good-looking content just got an owner's manual."

—Jason Miller
Senior Content Marketing Manager, LinkedIn

"Let's face it, writing is not optional for today's marketer. Ann's witty take on what works and what doesn't will help you master business writing and—more importantly—have fun while you're doing it!"

—Ardath Albee
B2B Marketing Strategist;
Author, *eMarketing Strategies for the Complex Sale*
and *Digital Relevance* (coming in 2015)

"Useful to the extreme, *Everybody Writes* is the first must-read book on the subject since Stephen King's *On Writing*. Bursting with ways to improve your short and long-form content, it's too good to be skimmed. This book should be included with every keyboard sold, like a combo pack of communication clarity. You'll be a better writer by page 15. By the end of this book, you're thinking about giving Steinbeck a run for his money. I passionately recommend *Everybody Writes*."

—Jay Baer
President, Convince & Convert;
Author, *Youtility*

"Finally, a sensible writing guide for a digital age! *Everybody Writes* is a unique blend of how-to-write rules and what-to-write revelations. Whether you are overhauling your everyday communication or sitting down to write a book, Ann Handley's irreverent style and inspirational wisdom will transform the way you write. Move over Strunk & White, *Everybody Writes* is the creative resource for a new generation."

—Andrew M. Davis
Author, *Brandscaping*

Everybody Writes

Everybody Writes

Your Go-To Guide to Creating Ridiculously Good Content

ANN HANDLEY

WILEY

For general information about our other products and services, please contact our Customer Care Department within the United States at (800) 762-2974, outside the United States at (317) 572-3993 or fax (317) 572-4002.

Wiley publishes in a variety of print and electronic formats and by print-on-demand. Some material included with standard print versions of this book may not be included in e-books or in print-on-demand. If this book refers to media such as a CD or DVD that is not included in the version you purchased, you may download this material at http://booksupport.wiley.com. For more information about Wiley products, visit www.wiley.com.

ISBN: 978-1-118-90555-5 (cloth)
ISBN: 978-1-118-90559-3 (ebk)
ISBN: 978-1-118-90561-6 (ebk)

Printed in the United States of America

V10003151_080718

To Evan, who always trusts his cape.

And to Caroline, who does things that scare her.

Beware of advice—even this.
—Carl Sandburg

Contents

Foreword

I came to writing reluctantly. My dirty little secret is that I got a *D* in college English.

I know, I know . . . so why am I writing a foreword for a book about writing? Because if I can learn to write well, so can you! And as the author of three best-selling books about communicating, I know how powerful great communication can be.

And anyway, do you really have a choice? Shouldn't you be writing better than you probably do now? There is a lot of barfy marketing content out there. It might be accurate, but it's often not interesting.

When I was talked into writing my first book, I set two objectives for myself:

1. To first believe I could do it, and . . .
2. To devour as many books about writing as possible.

That was in 2008. Man, I wish this book was around then.

This book inspires you to become a stronger writer. And it does so with style. In typical Handley fashion, every page will make you laugh, or at least smile. Ann is one of very few writers who can make me feel a cocktail of emotions in a single paragraph.

You should devour this book if you're a communicator, regardless of your title, position, years of experience, or job description. Because *everybody writes.*

If Strunk and White's *The Elements of Style* and Stephen King's *On Writing* had a baby, this would be it.

Be prepared to be delighted *and* to write better!

—**Nancy Duarte**
Owner, Duarte Design;
Author of *Slide:ology* and *Resonate*
Harvard Business Review Guide to Persuasive Presentations
Mountain View, CA

Acknowledgments

A h. So I see you, too, are one of those people who reads acknowledgments. Welcome, friend. You and I have a lot in common.

Writing a book is like birthing a Volkswagen. The process is about as pretty as you'd imagine that to be: it's long and arduous and you sweat a lot, and most of the work is done while crying.

My name might be on this book, but the following people helped—some of them considerably. You might call them midwives of sorts. But that might be taking the analogy a step too far.

Most special thanks to . . .

Kristina Halvorson, who gave me the title of this book and in exchange asks merely for all my love, money, and constant acknowledgment of her genius, which I gladly confer. With interest.

Vahe Habeshian, who put almost as much heart into this as I did. He's the world's best editor, among other things. And no, you cannot have his phone number.

My dear friend Nancy Duarte, for immediately saying yes to writing the foreword, which added a necessary, persistent pressure on me to get off the couch and finish this beast so she had something to actually write a foreword *to*.

Artist and number-one-son Evan W. H. Price, for the cover and interior illustrations, and also for being exactly the kind of person I could ever want him to be.

And also to . . .

Joe Chernov, for collaborating on an early iteration of Publishing Rules years ago, and for his consistently sound advice, smart sensibilities, and his ability to write circles around me.

Doug Kessler, for being an early reader of The Ugly First Draft—and still managing to say nice things about it. Also for his heart, soul, wisdom, and (especially) his humor.

Dane Sanders, who deserves top seeding in the World Cup of Encouraging Friends Playoffs. (If that's not a tournament, it should be.)

Andrew Davis, for his cheering and random emails that prodded me along when he probably didn't realize I needed it the most.

Lee Odden, for his consistent and generous support, smarts, and friendship.

Tim Washer, for being a great friend, conspirator, and collaborator for what seems like forever, or at least 20 years.

Kerry O'Shea Gorgone, for research help, legal expertise, high jinks, and shenanigans.

David Meerman Scott, for talking me through the framework of this book in a way that suddenly made it seem doable—instead of amorphous and hopeless and terrible. (This is also a good time to point out that he's done this for the second time in as many books.)

Jess Ostroff, for whatever the word is that means *things would literally fall apart without your expertise, supreme organization, and help with all the things.*

Wiley's Shannon Vargo, Peter Knox, and Elizabeth Gildea, who manage to possess equal measures of patience and impatience, and who also seem to have an uncanny sixth sense of which to apply when.

To *Entrepreneur* magazine, for permission to take bits and pieces of some of the material I wrote for my monthly column and reshape it here.

To my MarketingProfs family: It seems weird to refer to people I work with as a "family." But whatever. As my daughter Caroline tells me, "You be you, Mom. You be you."

To Facebook and Twitter, for making the writing of this book at least twice as long as it might have been otherwise.

And to the following for sharing their feedback and ideas generously and without expectation:

Jesse Noyes, Heidi Cohen, Jonathon Colman, Jason Miller, John Simmons, Richard Pelletier, Ahava Leibtag, Bernadette Jiwa, Andy Crestodina, Joe Pulizzi, Dan Lyons, Jay Baer, Ardath Albee, Sonia Simone, Brian Clark, Mitch Joel, Michael Brenner, Nick Westergaard, Paul Gillin, David B. Thomas, Corey O'Loughlin, Jill Foster, and the unparalleled C. C. Chapman.

Finally, is it pretentious to thank E. B. White?

The Elements of Style was a talisman to me when I was a college student learning to be a better writer; I clung to it like an infant lab monkey clings to its wire-frame mother, desperate to survive. (I still reread it every year or so.) White's quote in the Epilogue of *Everybody Writes* reminds me daily that anyone who waits for the perfect conditions to write won't ever actually create much of anything.

So, thanking a great writer I never met might indeed be pretentious. But some things just have to be said.

Introduction

Last Tuesday, for the first time in my life, I did a push-up. That wouldn't be remarkable for most of you, probably. It might even seem pathetic to most of you. But for me it was an occasion to celebrate, because it capped five months of hard work that followed a lifetime of resolutely thinking of myself as spectacularly incapable.

I hail from a stunningly unathletic family: most of us are more Eeyore than Seabiscuit; we are the ones picked last for the team, the ones who are afraid of the ball. And I was (quite literally) a 100-pound weakling. So the idea of my being capable of a push-up (or 5, or 10, or—maybe, eventually—50 or more!) seemed as improbable as my writing this in Russian.

Why am I telling you about that pathetic-but-epic push-up . . . in a book about writing and content creation and publishing?

Because learning to craft better content can involve nothing more than developing some necessary muscles. Right now you might not consider yourself much of a writer, or much of a content creator, just as I never considered myself someone who could drop and pump out a set of push-ups.

In our world, many hold a notion that the ability to write, or write well, is a gift bestowed on a chosen few. Writing well is considered a kind of art, linked murkily to muse and mysticism. That leaves us thinking there are two kinds of people: the writing haves—and the hapless, for whom writing well is a hopeless struggle, like trying to carve marble with a butter knife.

But I don't believe that, and neither should you. The truth is this: writing well is part habit, part knowledge of some fundamental rules, and part giving a damn. We are all capable of producing good writing. Or, at least, *better* writing. As David Carr of the *New York Times* says, "Writing is less about beckoning the muse than hanging in until the typing becomes writing."

So the two kinds of people are not the haves and the hapless. Instead, they are those who think they can write, and those who think they can't. (And, too often, both are wrong!)

In reality, most of us fall somewhere in the middle, capable of shedding mediocre writing to reveal something more inspired and reader-centric. We just need to train the necessary muscles.

But I'm Not a Writer

If you have a website, you are a publisher. If you are on social media, you are in marketing. And that means we are all writers.

Yeah, but who cares about writing anymore? In a time-challenged world dominated by short and snappy, by click-bait headlines and Twitter streams and Instagram feeds and gifs and video and Snapchat and YOLO and LOL and #tbt . . . does the idea of focusing on writing seem pedantic or ordinary?

And maybe a little useless, considering that an article (or so-called listicle) titled "13 Potatoes That Look Like Channing Tatum" on Buzz-Feed garners 2,000 tweets and 14,000 shares on Facebook?[1]

Actually, writing matters more now, not less. In an online world, our online words are our emissaries; they tell the world who we are, as user experience expert Beth Dunn puts it.[2]

Our writing can make us look smart or it can make us look stupid. It can make us seem fun, or warm, or competent, or trustworthy. But it can also make us seem humdrum or discombobulated or flat-out boring.

That means you've got to choose words well, and write with economy and style and honest empathy for your reader. And it means you put a new value on an often-overlooked skill in content marketing: how to write, and how to tell a true story really, really well. That's true whether you're writing a listicle or the words on a SlideShare deck or the words I'm using right here, right now. . . .

And so being able to communicate well in writing isn't just nice; it's a necessity. And it's also the oft-overlooked cornerstone of nearly all content marketing.

What Is Content?

So, yeah, what is *content?*

Content isn't limited to the text on our Web pages or product pages or blogs or e-mail newsletters. It's broader than the things we think of as marketing. Content is essentially everything your customer or prospect touches or interacts with—including your own online properties and Web pages and the experiences they offer, but also everything on any social channel (like Instagram, Twitter, Facebook, LinkedIn, YouTube, and so on).

Content is the entire user experience, says Kristina Halvorson, CEO of content strategy firm Brain Traffic and well-known speaker and author. Think of your content, then, as any medium through which you communicate with the people who might use your products or services.

Or, to paraphrase Mufasa the Lion King as he and his son Simba survey their kingdom at Pride Rock: "Everything the light touches is content."

I'm kidding. Of course Mufasa wasn't talking about content in the original quote, which is actually "Everything the light touches is our kingdom." But the concept loosely translates online as Everything Is Content.

And very often the core of that content—that user experience—is writing. Sometimes it's *literally* the experience—in the case of a blog post, e-book, white paper, Twitter post, or website text. And sometimes it's the basis of a visual experience—like that video or that SlideShare or PowerPoint presentation that began its life as a script, or that infographic that likely knits together data and text.

Yet in this content-driven environment, businesses often neglect or overlook words—much to their own detriment. Think of it this way: If a visitor came to your website without its branding in place (logo, tagline, and so on), would he or she recognize it as yours? If you stripped your branding from all your properties and lined up your words alongside a competitor's, would you recognize yourself? Would you stand out?

Words are indeed our emissaries and ambassadors, carrying important messages for us. "Words are a proxy . . . a stand-in for the things that we as people and we as companies want to convey to the world," Beth Dunn says.

So the question becomes: *Are you telling your story from your unique perspective, with a voice and style that's clearly all you?*

For businesses, good writing isn't merely any tool. It's the power tool they should be able to wield expertly, just as every respectable building contractor can use the Skilsaw he keeps in his truck.

Good writing is . . .

- ◆ *Often the foundation of good content* that gets noticed, no matter what form that content ultimately takes.
- ◆ *A mirror of good, clear, thinking* that's an antidote to the complexity that can sometimes characterize our business world. Amazon's Jeff Bezos reportedly relies on writing to hold effective meetings, requiring senior executives to read six-page narrative memos prior to in-person meetings, according to Janet Choi of iDoneThis, writing in *Fast Company*.[3]

    Choi cites a 2012 interview with Charlie Rose in which Bezos says: "When you have to write your ideas out in complete sentences and complete paragraphs, it forces a deeper clarity of thinking."[4] Choi adds: "Writing with a narrative structure rather than relying on messaging by numbers or bullet points also pushes people to think through problems within a fuller context."
- ◆ *The key to a customer-centric, intuitive, empathic point of view.* "Good writing . . . is a matter of developing the skills of intuitive psychology that are so important in every other aspect of social life: getting inside the heads of other people so that you can respect their needs and their wants," writes psychologist Steven Pinker in a Harvard publication.[5] (Thanks to Janet Choi for that link, too.)

Words matter. Your words (what you say) and style (how you say it) are your most cherished (and, yet, undervalued) assets.

Why We Need to Wage a War on Content Mediocrity (Or, Why This Book?)

Why? Three reasons . . .

1. *We have become a planet of publishers. Content Rules*, my first book (with C. C. Chapman), helped to ignite content-centric marketing, spreading the message of content as a cornerstone of marketing and championing its power to drive real business value. *Content Rules* became the best-selling book on content marketing, and (thus far) has been translated into nine languages.

In the four years since that book's publication, an over-whelming number of businesses have adopted a content-centric marketing mind-set: 93 percent of business-to-business companies (and 90 percent of business-to-consumer companies) say they are using content in their marketing mix, according to the 2014 annual survey produced by MarketingProfs and the Content Marketing Institute.[6]

Best-in-class marketers have set up the necessary structures and processes to consistently produce content. They've linked those efforts with strategic goals. They're upping content budgets. They're applying a variety of tactics—blogs, videos, webcasts, podcasts, and the like—12 tactics on average for B2B companies, 13 for B2C. They're using, on average, six social media platforms.

That's a lot of bustle over four years, isn't it?

Still, almost half of those marketers we surveyed (51 percent of B2C companies, and 47 percent of B2B companies) still struggle with how to create the kind of content that engages. At a fundamental level, we're all still struggling with how to create the kind of content that attracts customers.

Ours is a world where technology and social media have given us access and power: every one of us now has the awesome opportunity to own our own online publishing platforms—websites, blogs, email newsletters, Facebook pages, Twitter streams, and so on.

I don't use the phrase *awesome opportunity* lightly. The opportunity to change how we communicate with the people we are trying to reach, and what we communicate, is tremendous—yet we aren't taking full advantage of it.

Said another way: we are a planet of publishers, but many of us are littering the landscape with content crap, squandering the whopping opportunity we have to communicate directly with those we are trying to reach.

The challenge has shifted: we now grok the notion of content as a cornerstone of an online presence. Google and other search engines have made it clear that they'll love up the good stuff more than the regurgitated pabulum. Now let's focus on creating relevant, quality content experiences that our customers and prospects can trust.

We've embraced the idea of being publishers; the challenge that remains is the doing—the writing and publishing itself.

2. *Brevity and clarity matter more than ever.* Your awesome opportunity is also your competitor's awesome opportunity. It's also your colleague's, your friend's, your rival's, and that of the guy in the next cube who's neck-and-neck with you for that promotion.

   In other words, that opportunity has put new pressure on marketers and layered new requirements onto the marketing department, because there's a lot of competition clamoring to be heard. That's why it's important to write clearly and succinctly: to communicate your ideas and thoughts in a way that doesn't meander maddeningly; to respect the reader; to ensure that any content we produce doesn't come off as indulgent.

   I know this will sound harsh, but as someone who's been editing marketers for almost 20 years (first at ClickZ, and now at MarketingProfs), I assure you . . . an awful lot of content meandering goes on in articles, posts, PR pitches, and emails. I'm sorry to tell you so, but I also assure you there's love in my heart as I do.

3. *What matters now isn't storytelling; what matters is telling a true story well.* Marketing pundits increasingly talk up the importance of story and storytelling, and even I've crowed here about quality content.

   But those words all feel vague and amorphous, don't they? What's quality, exactly? And do we really want to be *storytelling*, with all the improvising and embellishing the word implies?

   Here's my take, after having been steeped in this new world of content marketing almost since its modern inception: quality, relevant content is less about storytelling; it's more about telling a true story *well.* Or, to paraphrase Jack Kerouac: "It ain't only whatcha write, it's also the *way* atcha write it."

   In our world, *quality* content means content that is packed with clear utility and is brimming with inspiration, and it has relentless empathy for the audience:

   • Utility means you clearly help your customers do something that matters to them—you help them shoulder their burdens, you ease their pain, or you help them make a decision.

- Inspiration means your content is inspired by data (more on this later) or it's creatively inspired (or both). It's fresh, different, well-written, well-produced, nicely designed—and it feels like it could come only from you.
- Empathy means you relentlessly focus on your customer. You view the entire world through his or her eyes—because, remember, *everything the light touches is content.*

I'm not much of a mathematician, but here's a handy, memorable formula that captures the sweet spot of your quality content. The multiplication signs are important, because if the value of any one of these things (Utility, Inspiration, or Empathy) is zero, then the sum of your content is a big fat zero, too. (Thanks to my friend and marketer Doug Kessler for the multiplication inspiration.):

Utility $\times$ Inspiration $\times$ Empathy = Quality Content

This is a good time to mention that quality in the context of your business doesn't necessarily mean writing with all the beauty or gravitas or heft of Hemingway or Michael Chabon or Joan Didion or George R. R. Martin or any other writer whose work you happen to admire.

Rather, I'm talking about getting to the essence of what makes those writers (or any writer!) great—whether you write novels or FAQ pages. And the key to that essence is a relentless empathy for your reader or audience.

One of the best, quality bits of content I ever encountered was a neatly designed guide to dishwasher repair I downloaded from an appliance website, because it delivered exactly what I needed with clear utility, inspiration, and empathy for the pain of having shards of a drinking glass caught in the drain hose.

Still Waiting. I Thought You Said You Were Going to Explain *Why This Book?*

Oh, right.

Although many excellent books on writing already exist, I've found that a lot of writing advice is really more aphorism than true advice.

They're entertaining to read and they can be a kind of rallying cry, but they aren't very how-to or prescriptive. (Which is always my bias. I like how-to advice. I don't know what to do with high-level, other than to wish it were more how-to.)

Alternatively, much of what passes for writing advice gets too deep in the weeds of writing construction. Great if you're looking to up your score on the SATs. Not so awesome if you just need some guidance on how not to sound like a total idiot when you craft this week's customer mailing.

What's harder to find is a book that functions for marketers as part writing and story guide, part instructional manual on the ground rules of ethical publishing, and part straight talk on some muscle-building writing processes and habits.

What's also hard to find is a book that distills some helpful ideas about the craft of content simply and (I hope) memorably, framed for the marketer and businessperson, as opposed to, say, the novelist or essayist or journalist.

I wrote this book because I couldn't find what I wanted—part writing guide, part handbook on the rules of good sportsmanship in content marketing, and all-around reliable desk companion for anyone creating or directing content on behalf of brands.

To that end, this book is separated into six sections; each deals with a different dimension of content:

- ◆ Part I, How to Write Better (and How to Hate Writing Less)—the latter for the recovering or traumatized writer—offers some handy scaffolding and blueprints for better thinking and writing.
- ◆ Part II, Grammar and Usage, discusses the stuff most people consider writing. It gives you some grammar rules and tools to help you choose better words and craft better sentences and paragraphs . . . to help you start flexing your content muscles.
- ◆ Next come Story Rules (Part III) and Publishing Rules (Part IV). The first provides some guidelines on elements that will infuse your content with heart and soul and integrity, and layer it with a warm blanket of trust. There's a lot to learn here from the ground rules of journalism and publishing, so those are covered in the part that follows.

- Next is 13 Things Marketers Write (Part V), which gives you a supertactical look at typical marketing tasks.
- And finally, Content Tools (Part VI) gives you a reference list of resources and paraphernalia to help you produce your best work.

There's also a lot that's *not* in this book, because it's not meant to be an exhaustive resource for the business of writing. Rather, it's meant to be your practical go-to guide, offering the most important and useful guideposts on the path toward better writing.

Content can be complex, but it's inherently easier to use your content as a driver of business when you start with a quality product, clear thinking, and good writing.

Stephen King calls fear the root of poor writing. But he points out (in his memoir *On Writing*): "Dumbo got airborne with the help of a magic feather . . . Just remember before you do that Dumbo didn't need the feather; the magic was in him."

The same is true of you. Of me. Of all of us. Like Dumbo, we just require the will and the courage and the inspiration and the gumption and the wits to start.

So, really, the question is not: *Are you telling your story from your unique perspective, with a style that's clearly all you?*

The real question is *Are you ready? Who's all in?*

Part I

Writing Rules: How to Write Better (and How to Hate Writing Less)

There is no one way to write—just as there is no one way to parent a child or roast a turkey. But there are terrible ways to do all three. And with each, you've got to have a basic understanding of the process before you begin. I'm going to assume you have that—you know enough, for example, to procure an oven and a pan before you begin to roast anything.

In other words, this book assumes that you are equipped with some very basic tools: a working knowledge of English (that means basic levels of grammar, spelling, usage, and punctuation). And I mean very basic: if you recognize that this is a sentence and not, say, a rhinoceros . . . we're good, and you can safely proceed knowing you aren't out of your depth. (In Part II, we'll talk about sharpening those tools in your content tool shed.)

It also assumes—or *hopes* is perhaps the better word—that you come with a bit of gung ho: an eagerness to become a better writer because you recognize that it matters, and because you've kicked to the curb the dumb notion that only an anointed few have the chops to be good writers.

Ta-Nehisi Coates, a senior editor at the *Atlantic*, spent a year teaching writing to MIT students. He later wrote, "I felt that the rigor of math had better prepared these kids for the rigor of writing. One of my students insisted that whereas in math you could practice and get better, in writing you either 'had it' or you didn't. I told her that writing was more like math then [sic] she suspected."[1]

In other words, good writing *can* be learned—the way trigonometry or algebra or balancing a balance sheet is a skill most of us can master. In an essay at the Neiman Journalism Lab, "How I Faced My Fears and Learned to Be Good at Math," Matt Waite writes: "The difference between good at math and bad at math is hard work. It's trying. It's trying hard. It's trying harder than you've ever tried before. That's it."[2]

The same is true about writing.

What you will read in this section is everything I know to be most important about writing: everything I have learned, collected, curated, and discovered over 25 years of writing and editing professionally (and a lifetime of writing for fun), distilled into the most important perspectives that I think can help all of us up our writing game.

This would be a good time to thank Neil Patel and Kathryn Aragon, coauthors of *The Advanced Guide to Content Marketing* (2013). Their guide helped me to conceptualize how I might present to you what I'd been doing—without putting much conscious thought into how I was doing it—for those 25 years. If you're looking for a handy reference for much more than writing, check it out in full at bit.ly/AdvancedGuide.

I hope that the rules in this section will help you to better organize and develop your writing—and to choose better words, craft better sentences, and consider things like cadence and flow, and many others that I'll stop specifying right now so you can just get to it . . . !

If you have never written—if you are an "adult-onset writer" who is perhaps recovering from some trauma that made you consider yourself an inept writer—this section provides some helpful processes and structures to help you get started.

If you've been writing for a while, here is some collected wisdom that may help you write better or more effectively.

And if you are an experienced writer, I hope you rediscover the glee and joy of honing a craft.

One final thing: I've organized this book as a series of so-called rules because I wanted to offer useful and (I hope) memorable how-tos. I also wanted to differentiate these ideas from the general motivational aphorisms that pass for most writing advice. Part I is a gaggle of helpful how-tos specific to the writing process and organization of a piece (it's less boring than it sounds), as well as advice for livelier writing. Part II will cover grammar and usage, framed for a marketing audience.

In any case, these "rules" are intended to be functional *tools*, not prescriptive *rules*. So, as we wrote (in a different context) in *Content Rules*, any rules here are less hard-and-fast writing rules than they are a handy set of guidelines. Think of them more as bumpers on a bowling lane that nudge the ball away from the gutter and greatly increase the odds that the ball you throw will land a strike.

Of course, you can break the rules (or ignore the tools) as you wish. Isn't every rule made to be broken? Doesn't every rule have an exception? You might be a kind of content MacGyver who wackily crafts beautiful content out of a metaphorical paper clip and roll of Scotch tape. That's totally great—in fact, I hope you do! But, first, you have to know what rules to break (or what tools to ignore).

1

Everybody Writes

I want to tell you that the key to taking your writing muscles from puny to brawny is to write every day. That writing is a habit, not an art. It is the former—and I'll talk about that in a minute. But before I do, let's reframe this business of writing.

As you think of developing a writing habit, realize that you probably already *do* write every day. You write emails; you post to Facebook, Twitter, or Instagram; you comment on blogs. Recognize all that posting for what it is: writing. And reframe it as a legit aspect of your daily workout—in the same way always taking the stairs becomes, over time, part of a fitness regimen.

I hope you'll consider this first rule a kind of call to arms to improve *all* of your communications, rather than just the stuff we traditionally think of as "content." Embrace the idea (as I said in the Introduction) that your words are your Web currency: they are a proxy, a stand-in for the important things you want to convey to your customers, and the world.

I want your readers and followers and audience to enjoy your words more, and I want you to maybe even feel a little proud of them.

But getting to that point requires—in all of us—a crucial shift: viewing the words we use as an important piece of who we (and our companies) are online. First, though, we have to overcome what holds us back from being writers: a combination of fear, lethargy, and a lack of confidence or knowledge (or both).

"If you want to be a writer you must do two things above all others: read a lot and write a lot," Stephen King writes in his book *On Writing*. He is talking to those who want to make their living as he does, writing books. But, in our world, we're all already writing and reading a lot. Every day.

I am a writer. You are a writer. *Everybody writes*.

2

Writing Is a Habit, Not an Art

We're tempted to think that writing is an art, that only an anointed lucky few can do it well. But that's an excuse—a justification that lets the lazy among us off the hook for being the communication equivalent of a couch potato: flabby, unmotivated, inarticulate. But the truth is that the key to being a better writer is, essentially, to be a more productive one. Or more simply, the key to being a better writer is to write.

You'd think that great writers would have special inspiration or contrived stimuli to boost their output—not unlike what poet, humorist, and educator Taylor Mali hilariously suggested in his deadpan response to a question about his favorite place to write:

> *I'd love to say I have handmade Japanese paper and a 200-year-old fountain pen . . . and every morning, after making love, for the third time . . . I go running, for about five miles . . . if I'm feeling lazy.*
>
> *[At] the top of our house, there's an old cupola, and I watch the sunrise up there, in the nude, and I write my poems longhand. I'm right-handed but I force myself to use my left hand, because I find it makes me more creative. And I write, in Latin, because it forces the brain to work in a new way—backwards, like Hebrew . . .*

But, really, Mali adds,

> *I just sit in front of my computer.*[1]

Many of the world's most brilliant writers stressed regular routines and schedules for writing. Maya Angelou, Ernest Hemingway, Charles

Dickens, and Oliver Sacks kept regular hours to cultivate creative rhythms. They might've had certain quirks (it's true that Hemingway wrote standing up, and Maya Angelou kept a room in a budget hotel to escape the distractions of her domestic life), but many kept schedules and routines that look as ordinary and predictable as those in anyone else's life.[2]

Here's a peek at what the prolific Ben Franklin called his daily scheme:

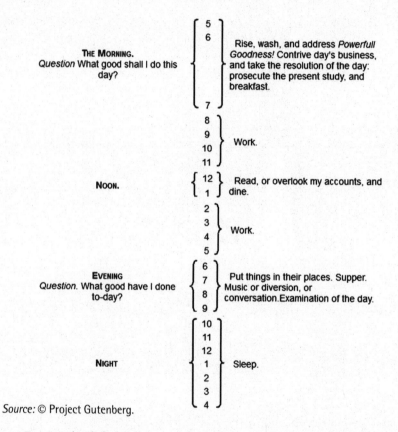

Source: © Project Gutenberg.

Ben's schedule looks an awful lot like everyday work. Like routine. Like a conventional pattern you'd see from someone punching a clock in a factory.

Well . . . that's because it is. Becoming a better writer—working the muscle—takes some commitment to simply show up, not unlike the commitment I kept with my gym trainer, Dorothy. Both writing and strength training can feel awkward and a little painful at first: I felt like a total poser donning spandex and sneakers, and I felt idiotic grunting under the weight of barbells that seemed sized for an undernourished eight-year-old. But the point is to keep at it, even when it's uncomfortable and you'd rather quit.

Simply put, the key to being a better writer is to write.

Make a regular habit of it, because as author Gretchen Rubin writes, "Habits are the invisible architecture of everyday life."[3] In this case, habit lends the necessary scaffolding to support better writing.

"Write like crap if you have to. But write every day. Keep the streak alive," said Beth Dunn, a user-experience editor for HubSpot, during a talk on how to become a "writing god" at her company's 2013 user event in Boston.[4]

So what kind of prescription works?

Set aside time each day when you're freshest. I'm freshest first thing in the morning, before distractions hijack my day. For you it might be different. You've been living with yourself long enough to know what time of day would work for you, so I'll leave that in your hands.

Don't write a lot. Just write often. The advice to write often is from author Jeff Goins, who points out on his site, GoinsWriter.com, "Spending five hours on a Saturday writing isn't *nearly* as valuable as spending 30 minutes a day every day of the week. Especially when you're just getting started."

I love how Jeff talks about why that daily part is important: He says habits "practiced once a week aren't habits at all. They're *obligations.*"

"And let's not kid ourselves here," he adds. "If you're doing something once a week, it's probably only a matter of time before you stop doing it altogether."[5]

There are no shortcuts to becoming a better writer. So show up at your desk and get to it. Daily.

3

Shed High School Rules

This past spring, College Board officials announced sweeping revisions to the SAT college entrance exam. Key among the changes was that the dreaded five-paragraph essay portion of the test will become entirely optional in 2016.

MIT professor Les Perelman has long been a harsh critic of the essay. In a *New York Times Magazine* piece, Perelman talked about research he conducted that highlighted the folly of the essay, finding that essay length, fancy words, and a sprinkling of random, esoteric facts all correlate with high essay scores. In that piece and in a subsequent interview on NPR, Perelman recalled how he coached 16 students who were retaking the test after having received mediocre scores on the essay section. The *Times* reporter Todd Balf writes:

> He told them that details mattered but factual accuracy didn't. "You can tell them the War of 1812 began in 1945," he said. He encouraged them to sprinkle in little-used but fancy words like "plethora" or "myriad" and to use two or three preselected quotes from prominent figures like Franklin Delano Roosevelt, regardless of whether they were relevant to the question asked.

Perelman encouraged them to be long-winded and to fill up the entire test booklet—and the margins and back pages—if they could. The result: 15 of his 16 pupils scored higher than the ninetieth percentile on the essay when they retook the exam, Perelman said. And—most tellingly—he added (in a subsequent interview on Boston's

WBUR): "and then I told them never to write that way again!" Because, he said, "no one is actually learning anything about writing."[1]

Many of us learned in high school to write what is commonly known as the five-paragraph essay, similar in format to the soon-to-be-former SAT test. It goes something like this:

1. *Introduction.* The introduction is a thesis statement or a kind of mini-outline of what the essay will cover.
2. *Body Paragraph One.* Body paragraph one should include the strongest argument, most compelling example, or cleverest point that dramatizes your thesis. The first sentence of this paragraph should include the so-called reverse hook, which ties in with the transitional hook at the end of the introductory paragraph. The topic for this paragraph should be covered in its first or second sentence. That topic should relate to the thesis statement in the introductory paragraph. The last sentence in this paragraph should include a transitional hook to tie into the second paragraph of the body.
3. *Body Paragraph Two.* Body paragraph two should include the second-strongest argument, compelling example, or cleverest point.
4. *Body Paragraph Three.* Body paragraph three should include the third (or weakest) argument, example, or point.
5. *Conclusion.* Your conclusion should be a restatement of the thesis statement that uses some of the original words to echo— but not duplicate—the opening paragraph, as well as a summary of the three main points.

This might be a perfectly fine structure to help guide a classroom of young writers in middle school. (Some educators actually debate its use, but that's a topic for them to debate, not me.) The problem with its use beyond that, though, is that it's so structured and formulaic that it's boring to write and boring to read. Worse still, it implies there is just one right way to write and that other approaches to writing are wrong.

There is no one way to write—just as there is no one way to parent a child or roast a turkey.

What you learned in school might've once been a helpful guide-post. But it's time to let go. As Janis says in the movie *Mean Girls*: "That's the thing with five-paragraph essays. You think everybody is in love with them when actually everybody HATES them!"

Actually, Janis was talking about the school's mean girls—The Plastics. Not essays. But same dif.

4

Regard Publishing as a Privilege

The best companies don't just churn out regular blog posts with the heavy-handedness of an orphanage doling out gruel. Rather, they put the needs of their audiences first; they regard the ability to create content as something of a privilege, as my friend Tom Fishburne of Marketoonist.com often notes.

Does it sound quaint to suggest that publishing is a privilege instead of some kind of perceived right?

I don't think so. Instead, I think it's a necessary mind-set that creates a breeding ground for great content. Inherent in that attitude is that you value your relationship with your audience, and that you put their needs first.

I don't say that lightly: every bit of content you create should be to please the customer or prospect—*not* your boss or client. More on that in a few.

We all have easy access to a publishing platform and a potential audience. We all have great power to influence, educate, entertain, and help—but also to annoy, irritate, and . . . sometimes . . . fritter away our opportunity entirely.

So the challenge for companies is to respect their audiences and deliver what the audience needs in a way that's useful, enjoyable, and inspired. The challenge is to also keep it tight, as Tim Washer, who produces video for Cisco, espouses. That means *clarity, brevity,* and *utility.*

Brevity doesn't mean bare bones or stripped down. Take as long as you need to tell the story. (The length of content is dictated by the kind of content you're creating.) The notion of brevity has more to do with cutting fat, bloat, and things that indulge the writer and don't respect the reader's time. Keep it tight.

Make it clear. Don't make the reader work hard to understand you. Develop pathological empathy for the reader. (More on that in a minute too.) And finally, make it useful. Readers will read what you write only if something is in it for them.

Write, rewrite, edit. As content strategist Jonathon Colman, who works for Facebook, told me: "Start with empathy. Continue with utility. Improve with analysis. Optimize with love."

5

Place the Most Important Words (and Ideas) at the Beginning of Each Sentence

We tend to junk up the beginning of our sentences with modifiers and qualifiers, making the reader work harder to discern what, exactly, we are saying. It might sound remedial to say that each sentence should begin with the subject (the actor) and verb (the action), but it's the easiest way to buff up bad writing to make it more appealing.

The first words of every sentence should make a friendly first impression to encourage the reader to keep going—much the way a favorable first impression at a party encourages conversation (as opposed to, say, desperate glances around the room to find some other opportunity).

Here's what I mean.

This is the first sentence of an introductory paragraph of a Centers for Disease Control and Prevention style guide: "According to the National Assessment of Adult Literacy (NAAL), released in 2006 by the U.S. Department of Education, 30 million adults struggle with basic reading tasks."[1]

The primary idea in that sentence is that millions of people are not fully literate; everything else in it is secondary. The primary idea—the important words—should be placed at the beginning. So:

"Thirty million adults struggle with reading, according to the National Assessment of Adult Literacy (NAAL) report, released in 2006 by the U.S. Department of Education."

(Ironically, the guide is titled *Simply Put*, though much of it is not put simply at all.)

Also from *Simply Put* (ignore, for the moment, the incorrect use of the semicolon):

"It is important to remember; however, that even those with higher health literacy skills want health information that is understandable, meaningful to them, and easy to use."

What happens when you scrap the stuff at the beginning of that sentence ("It is important to remember; however, that . . .")? You eliminate distractions, and you highlight what's important—without changing the meaning: "Even those with higher health literacy skills want health information that is understandable, meaningful to them, and easy to use."

Here are some phrases to avoid at the start of a sentence:

♦ According to . . .
♦ There is a . . .
♦ It is [important, critical, advised, suggested, and so on] . . .
♦ In my opinion . . .
♦ The purpose of this [email, post, article] is . . .
♦ In 2014 [or any year] . . .
♦ I think [believe] that . . .

You can tack them onto the end, or insert them somewhere in the middle—if you must use them at all.

6

Follow a Writing GPS

At times, writing can feel like birthing a Volkswagen to me (I've even used that metaphor on occasion to describe writing this book). The writer Andre Dubus (*House of Sand and Fog*) has described writing as inching your way along a very dark, very long tunnel: you can make out the next few feet in front of you, but you're not quite certain where you'll end up or when you'll get there.

What helps with the uncertainty and enormity of the task is to start with some kind of process to guide the way.

When I was in middle school and learning to be a better writer, though, the focus was purely on the end product. My teachers emphasized the final paper versus the rough drafts and scratch notes that preceded it. In other words, they were more interested in seventh-grade Ann's delivering an essay on *The Red Badge of Courage*'s Henry Fleming than they were in *how* that essay came to be sitting on their desk at all.

Or so it seemed at that time. Maybe process was part of the curriculum (*Ms. Dolan, if you are reading this now, please clarify for me*). But I don't recall much emphasis on the necessary checkpoints along the way to that final piece—the beacons that guide the entire effort.

Process is one of those things that in many parts of life I consider hopelessly boring and mind-numbing. Like peeling the skins of raw tomatoes. Or scrubbing dirt from beets. But in writing, process is necessary, because you *need* a road map to get you to where you need to be.

Essentially, it's a kind of writing GPS that gets you from discombobulated thoughts to a coherent, cogent piece of writing that others can understand and appreciate.

What follows is the 12-step process for any new, longer text you might produce—blog posts, e-books, white papers, site content, and the like. It's the process I use to write any blog post that appears on MarketingProfs or AnnHandley.com, and I use it to create my monthly column in *Entrepreneur* magazine. Also, I've used it to cobble together the bones of video scripts and presentations, as well as longer memo-style emails.

You'll notice that some of the themes here are also discussed elsewhere in this book. Serving the reader and not the writer, for one. Finding credible sources or data to support your point of view, for another. And creating The Ugly First Draft (TUFD).

But having a big-picture view of the process, or an outline of it, is useful. As we'll talk about in The Ugly First Draft section, good writing takes planning and preparation; it doesn't just emerge, fully formed, out of the head of Zeus. Or your own head, for that matter.

(You can dig further into some of the 12 steps, as noted. Or you can simply rely on this *CliffsNotes* version. Your call.)

1. *Goal.* What's your business goal? What are you trying to achieve? Anything you write should always be aligned with a larger (business or marketing) goal—even an individual blog post.

   The key here is that you care about what you're writing: you can try to fake it, but your readers will be allergic to your insincerity. Why does that matter? Because if you don't care about what you're writing about, no one will.

   Let's say your goal is this: I want to drive awareness of and interest in the launch of our incredibly cool new collaborative editing software because we want to sell more of it.

2. *Reframe: put your reader into it.* Reframe the idea to relate it to your readers. Why does it matter to them? What's in it for them? Why should they care? What's the clear lesson or message you want them to take away? What value do you offer them? What questions might they have? What advice or help can you provide?

My friend Tim Washer of Cisco refers to this reframing as giving your audience a gift: how can you best serve them, with a mind-set of generosity and giving?

To get to the heart of this reframing, I ask: so what? And then answer, because. Repeat the so what/because query and response string as many times as necessary, until you've exhausted any ability to come up with an answer. Or until you're questioning things best left to the philosophers. As in:

> I want to drive interest and awareness in the launch of our new collaborative editing software.
>
> *So what?*
>
> Because our new text editor makes it stupid easy in three specific ways for those of you without a geek gene to easily collaborate from remote locales, without overwriting each other's stuff or losing earlier versions.
>
> *So what?*
>
> Because that's a pain to deal with, and it causes a lot of frustration and suffering for collaborative, virtual teams.
>
> *So what?*
>
> Because pain . . . it hurts. And suffering is . . . umm . . . bad.

You get the idea.

Express your reframed idea as a clear message. In this case, something like this:

> *Our new text editor makes it stupid easy in three specific ways for those of you without a geek gene to easily work together from remote locales, without overwriting each other's stuff or losing earlier versions, which makes for happier, less frustrated collaborators. And you'll get your work done faster, with less wasted effort.*

Then put that at the top of the page, like a bonfire on the beachhead, to remind you where you're headed.

3. *Seek out the data and examples.* What credible source supports your main idea? Are there examples, data, real-world

stories, relevant anecdotes, timely developments, or new stories you can cite? (See specific advice about using data in Part IV.)

Don't discount your own experience; at the same time, don't rely exclusively on it. Use yourself as one of your sources if you have relevant experience (many writers in the *New Yorker* do so frequently; see Rule 17). That works, because "the more personal you are, the more universal you become," says Chip Scanlan, Poynter.org's writing advice columnist.

"The writer who uses herself as a source and resource has the greatest chance of connecting with the largest audience," Chip points out. "[A]sk yourself: What do I think about this story? What do I know about it?"

You'll want to research your topic, of course. But "the smart writers I know start out by tapping into their own private stock first," Chip says.[1]

In our example, ask: Is there research that quantifies the problem? Who else has dealt with catastrophes or successes? Could you talk to those people or organizations to get their firsthand horror stories and advice? Also, what's been your own experience?

4. *Organize*. What structure helps communicate your point? Some options are a list, a how-to guide, and a client narrative. Organize the outline or general architecture that suits that type of story best. (See Rule 8.)

5. *Write to one person*. Imagine the one person you're helping with this piece of writing. And then write directly to that person (using *you*, as opposed to using *people* or *they*).

Connect your reader to the issue you're writing about (again, why does it matter to him or her?), perhaps by relaying a scenario or telling a story. Put your reader (or someone just like him or her) into your story right up front—because you want the reader to recognize and relate to an issue. (See Rule 17 for more.)

6. *Produce The Ugly First Draft*. Producing The Ugly First Draft is basically where you show up and throw up. Write badly. Write as if no one will ever read it. (Stephen King calls this "writing with the door closed.") Don't worry about grammar, complete

sentences, or readability. Don't fret about spelling or usage. You'll tackle all that later. For now, just get that TUFD down.

By the way, this show-up-and-throw-up phase is often where many bloggers end the process. But you won't do that—because you have respect both for your writing and for your reader.

7. *Walk away.* Walking away is self-explanatory. You don't need to actually go for a walk, of course. Just put some distance between your first draft and the second.

How much distance depends on you. I try to put a day between my own (usually spectacularly ugly!) TUFD and the next step, because that amount of time seems to let my thinking season and mature. I feel better prepared to slap those words around a little, willing them to shape up on the page.

I don't always have the luxury of that long a fermentation period—and if a piece is tied to a news story you might not either. So work with what you've got. But at least try to get out of the building—maybe grab a coffee or a slice of pie or something.

8. *Rewrite.* Shape that mess into something that a reader wants to read. In your head, swap places with your reader as you do so. (See Rule 10.)

9. *Give it a great headline or title.* See Rule 69 for more on writing irresistible headlines.

10. *Have someone edit.* Ideally, the person who edits your piece will have a tight grip on grammar, usage, style, and punctuation. Like a bona fide editor. (See Rule 24.)

11. *One final look for readability.* Does your piece look inviting, alluring, easy to scan? With short paragraphs and bold subheads? Are your lists numbered or bulleted? For the most part, chunky chunks of text feel impenetrable and don't convey energy and movement. In other words, bulky text doesn't look like much fun to read. (See Rule 25.)

12. *Publish, but not without answering one more reader question: what now?* Don't leave your readers just standing awkwardly in the middle of the dance floor after the music stops. What do you want them to do next?

- Check out other resources?
- Sign up to hear more?
- Register for an event or a free trial?
- Buy something?

Consider the order of the steps in this outlined writing process merely a suggestion. You can toss them around and follow them in any order you wish—perhaps you like to barf your first draft onto the page incoherently (Rule 6) and *then* organize your writing into something more cogent (Rule 4). That's fine; it's completely at your discretion. There is no one way to write, remember?

(The only order I wouldn't suggest is backward, because that's just dumb.)

7

The More the Think, the Easier the Ink

"It's not the ink—it's the think," wrote *New Yorker* cartoon editor Robert Mankoff, when asked about the secret to drawing the magazine's iconic cartoons.

"As cartoon editor, I'm often asked how to get ideas for cartoons by people who want to submit them to the *New Yorker*," Mankoff wrote on the *New Yorker* blog. "There really is no trick—you just have to think of them."[1]

Mankoff's think-before-ink mnemonic is easily applied to the first and second GPS checkpoints of writing too: distilling an idea, and reframing it for your reader. (An aside—it would also be a great tagline for a tattoo studio.)

Mankoff's deliberately oversimplified answer reveals a fundamental truth about cartoons, and about any content: the more you think about what you want to say, and plan for it, the easier it is to say.

Figuring out *what* you want to say before you figure out *how* to say it seems an obvious first step. But many writers tend to shortchange that step—they instead charge straight at the water and wade in, slogging through the surf until pretty soon they're out of their depth and they're flailing around wondering how they ended up there at all.

"If I'm really struggling, it's usually not about the writing—it's about the thinking: I just don't really have the story down yet," Doug Kessler told me. "So more research or groping with the outline can unstick me.

"If I do know the story but I'm just dopey or sleepy or grumpy (my preferred dwarf-personas), I give it a rest, get some sleep or take a shower or pound some Diet Coke or take a walk," Doug added. "An hour with a fresh mind is worth five hours of fog."

So, before you begin the writing, be sure you know the purpose or mission or objective of every piece of content that you write. What are you trying to achieve? What information, exactly, are you trying to communicate? And why should your audience care?

A caveat: some writers—including me—write as a way to figure out *what* we think. You, too, might develop your thoughts through writing, and you might not always have a clear sense of what exactly you want to say until you're knee-deep in the water. In that case the think-before-ink idea might seem counterproductive, but it's not. I'm talking about having a general sense of the key point or direction of the piece, as well as how to relate to the audience, even if that general sense is not fully fleshed out in your own head before you start.

Often the flailing comes about because we haven't thought about an idea enough to find that key point—in which case we haven't thought through the supporting arguments we want to make to shore up that point. So it helps to first jot down thoughts to try to find a focus and points in support of it (see Rule 8).

Think before ink means finding your key point by asking three questions about every bit of content you're creating. We talked a lot about this process in Rule 6, but to recap:

Why am I creating this? What's my objective?

What is my key take on the subject or issue? What's my point of view?

And, finally, the critical *so what?-because* exercise: why does it matter to the people you are trying to reach?

In some cases that key point becomes the headline. Sometimes during the writing phase I think of something better to use as a headline. But, still, that exercise lends the necessary focus.

And, by the way, this approach applies equally well to blog posts or presentations or books. You might have more supporting points in a book or longer piece of content, but you should still be able to describe the key point in a single sentence. As I'm writing now, the guiding sentence at the top of my page is this: *A handbook for businesses to create better content with more care and discretion, because we live in a world where we are all writers.* It's not very artful, but it's getting the job done.

Shakespeare probably wrote Hamlet with this sentence at the top of his parchment: *Angsty, brooding Danish prince goes nuts (or does he?) but murders many, including the creepy uncle who had killed his father and married his mother.*

Or maybe not. But it's fun to think he did.

8

Organize. Relax, You've Got This

Good writing is like math: it has logic and structure. It feels solid to the reader: the writer is in control, having taken on the heavy burden of making a piece of writing clear and accessible. It might not follow a formula, exactly. But there's a kind of geometric architecture to it.

There's no single way to organize a piece of writing. What works for me (as I said previously) is a single line at the top of the page that sums up the main point I'm trying to make. Then I list some key points that relate to or support my bigger idea. Then I go back and expand on those ideas in another sentence or two, creating paragraphs. Then I move the paragraphs around, adding transitions between them to create a smooth flow.

In other words, I make a list, because it feels less intimating to make a list than it does to write. (Do you ever feel stumped about where to begin a shopping list? Me neither.)

Your process might be different. Rather than a list, you might use mind mapping, a flowchart, note cards, sticky notes, a pen and paper, a whiteboard and some fat markers, or whatever. J. K. Rowling sussed out the first *Harry Potter* novel using graphing paper and a ball-point pen.

Chicago-based marketer Andy Crestodina writes an outline of a piece and then makes the main points its headers. Then he fleshes out the outline in a kind of fill-in-the-blank exercise. For him, "great writing isn't written, as much as assembled," Andy told me.

"I almost always write an outline, even if it's only a scribble on a piece of paper," Doug Kessler said in an interview with me. "It helps me plan the arc of the story and the flow, so I always know where I'm headed."

Similarly, Chris Penn, who writes prolifically (almost daily) about marketing and social media on his *Awaken Your Superhero* blog, showed me recently how he fleshed out nine sentence fragments into a 400-word blog post that related business to martial arts.

So this:

You understand what to do, unpack the bottle.

A lot of frameworks and models are shorthand like the heart Sutra.

To make the most of it you need to unpack it and take it apart.

This is exactly what we do in the martial arts with our kata.

Our routines are unpacked at each move study.

By doing this with marketing frameworks and models as bottles we can understand what it is we are supposed to do with each individual portion of a funnel.

This is operationalizing a big idea that you take apart until we understand how it actually works.

This is also how to detect which are genuine big ideas and which are bullshit.

You unpack an idea that is bullshit and you'll find nothing to operationalize.

Became this when it was published later on his blog:

How to Assess a Big Marketing Idea

See if this sounds familiar: marketing thought leader X publishes a new paper with a grand Big Idea, complete with fancy infographic and a chart or framework that is both dazzlingly complex and slightly intimidating. Whether you like said thought leader or not, you wonder whether their Big Idea is actually worth pursuing, or whether it's just a bunch of hot air, and pursuing it would be a waste of time and resources.

(continued)

(*continued*)

I've been in that situation plenty of times over the years. I've seen lots of Big Ideas, lots of fancy frameworks, lots of infographics whose design budget probably eclipsed some peoples' annual income. To figure out what's the real deal and what's BS, I borrowed an idea from the martial arts.

In the martial arts tradition I practice, we have lots of Big Ideas called *kata*. Loosely translated from Japanese, the word means form or routine, in the sense of something you practice. Each one is a Big Idea, how to win in a certain way under a specific set of adverse circumstances.

My teacher, Mark Davis of the Boston Martial Arts Center, taught us that to learn and master a *kata*, you have to break it apart and study each of the pieces. How does a wrist lock in the middle of *Batsu Gi kata* work outside of those particular circumstances? Can you make it work versus a punch? A knife? You operationalize each piece of the *kata* until you know how it works; when you put it back together, you truly understand it.

This methodology, which has served me well for over two decades, is one you can use for evaluating any thought leader's Big Idea. If you read about some new framework or concept, see if you can break it apart into operational pieces. See if you can transform the Big Idea into little things that you can implement. If you can, then you know the Big Idea has wheels—it's something that can be tested, evaluated in components, and used to make change in your business at both tactical and strategic levels.

If you try to take apart a Big Idea and find that there's little or nothing you can operationally implement, then you know the Big Idea is either a complete mismatch for your organization, or it might be full of hot air entirely. Try it with any of the Big Ideas of the day and see if you can turn them into Little Things To Do!

Source: Christopher S. Penn, "How to Assess a Big Marketing Idea," *Awaken Your Superhero* (blog), April 2, 2104, www.christopherspenn.com/2014/04/how-to-assess-a-big-marketing-idea.

Your preferred method for organizing a piece doesn't matter. The point is to keep yourself focused and organized via some set framework so you don't meander all over the place.

Working from a prescription offers some guideposts to follow and gives you momentum toward what's next.

How can you organize a blog post or article? Whatever its substance, consider what form you want it to take. Here are 15 approaches to framing your writing, adapted from Boston-based writing coach Paul Gillin. Here he uses online privacy as a sample topic:

Organizing a Blog Post or Article

1. *Quiz.* Test Your Privacy IQ
2. *Skeptic.* You Don't Control Your Privacy Anymore
3. *Explainer.* The Online Privacy Debate in Plain English
4. *Case study.* How One Person Got Control Over Privacy
5. *Contrarian.* Why Online Privacy Concerns Are Overblown
6. *How-to.* Five Steps to Improving Online Privacy
6½. *Quick How-to.* Three Stupid Simple Things You Can Do to Keep Your Profile Private
7. *How NOT to.* Five Ways to Compromise Your Online Privacy
8. *First person.* My Personal Privacy Horror Story
9. *Comparison.* How Privacy Protection Services Measure Up
10. *Q&A.* Five Common Questions About Online Privacy with Edward Snowden
11. *Data.* Are Privacy Problems Worsening? Yes, Says Survey
12. *Man on the street.* Experts Offer Opinions on the State of Online Privacy
13. *Outrageous.* Why Online Privacy Is an Oxymoron
13½. *BuzzFeed-style outrageous (not advised, but good for a laugh!).* This Woman Insists Online Privacy Is a Joke, and You Won't Believe What Happened Next

(continued)

(*continued*)

14. *Insider secrets.* The One Thing You Need to Know About Your Online Privacy

15. *Literary treatment.* Online privacy haiku, epic narrative poem, comic book treatment, or whatever else your imagination can muster!

Source: Paul Gillin, "Create Stuff They've Just Gotta Read: How to Write for #SocialNetworks," presentation at MarketingProfs Digital Marketing World, December 13, 2013, www.marketingprofs.com/events/24/dec2013/545/.

9

Embrace The Ugly First Draft

So now that you've figured out what to write—and generally how it'll go—just write. Or, rather, write badly and create a first draft: The Ugly First Draft (TUFD) I talked about earlier.

TUFD isn't a pass you give yourself to produce substandard work. But it is a necessary part of the process of creating above standard work.

In Greek mythology, the goddess Athena was the favorite daughter of Zeus. She was born not in the usual way; rather, she emerged from his forehead fully grown and armed.

Much of writing paralysis is the result of expecting too much of ourselves the first time out. Sowing letters onto the blank page and expecting something strong and powerful and fully formed—the content version of Athena—to emerge is unrealistic. Unless you are some kind of deity, that's not going to happen.

Very often, the people you think of as good writers are terrible writers on their first drafts. But here's their secret: They are *excellent editors* of their own work.

So embrace The Ugly First Draft as necessary. As painful and depressing as it might be to write badly—at least you're writing, you're getting the mess out of your head and onto the screen or paper. Then, when you get back to it, you can start shaping it into something more respectable.

Recognize that brilliance—or anything close to it—comes on the rewrite. That implies that there *is* a rewrite, of course. And there should be.

As writing teacher Don Murray said, "The draft needs fixing, but first it needs writing."[1]

Here's a timeline to keep in mind:

1. *Barf up TUFD.* Think about what you want to say (think before ink!) and add your guiding bullet points or sentences at the top of the page.

   Jot down your key ideas as they come to you in whatever order they come.

   Don't worry about forming full (or even coherent!) sentences. Don't worry about finding the right words. Lowercased words, misspelling, poor grammar, awkward phrasing, subject-verb disagreements so violent they are practically fistfights . . . Let it all happen. You can fix all that stuff later. You're unleashing ideas here as opposed to really writing.

   If you get stuck, think about what's sticking. Do you need more research? More examples? Another point?

   Inserting "need a better example here" or "could use a research stat" or "something-something that supports that point" or "funnier anecdote" is more than legit during this phase.

   Reread what you've written only to remind yourself of what else you wanted to say, or to add some flesh to the bones of your terrible writing. (Even if it's rotting, smelly, walking-dead flesh.)

   Ban self-slandering remarks. Don't beat yourself up by saying things like I'm a crappy writer or this is awful. TUFD isn't for anyone to see but you. It's the content equivalent of staying home alone in your jammies all day and eating peanut butter straight from the jar. Revel in it. There's no one around to judge.

2. *Walk away.* You'll feel some relief at getting the first draft out—but you might also feel frustrated by your TUFD. So this is a good time to walk away from each other. Get some space so that you can both cool off a bit. Grab the dog's leash and go for a walk, meet friends for lunch, whatever. Just put some distance between you two. Then, when you get back to it, you'll be fresh and (hopefully) less agitated.

   As I said in Rule 6, I like to put a lot of distance between me and my ugliness. I try to not look at my TUFD again until the next day.

3. *Rewrite.* When you do get back to it, you might be horrified. You might shield your eyes the way nineteenth-century London recoiled from John Hurt in the movie *The Elephant Man*. But you will find things you like that you can upcycle. In other words, take the best parts of the draft and use them in your final product. How to do that is covered next.

10

Swap Places with Your Reader

"The reader doesn't turn the page because of a hunger to applaud," said longtime writing teacher Don Murray.[1]

Good writing serves the reader, not the writer. It isn't self-indulgent. Good writing anticipates the questions that readers might have as they're reading a piece, and it answers them.

Some writers adopt this mind-set during the initial writing phase. But this perspective is especially helpful on the rewrite or edit, once the first draft is out of your head and onto the page.

Swap places with your reader. Be a skeptic of your own work. Get out of your own head, and into your reader's or your customer's. Relentlessly, unremittingly, obstinately think of things from your readers' point of view, with empathy for the experience you are giving them.

In his essay "Politics and the English Language," George Orwell wrote: "A scrupulous writer, in every sentence that he writes will ask himself at least four questions, thus: What am I trying to say? What words will express it? What image or idiom will make it clearer? Is this image fresh enough to have an effect?

And he will probably ask himself two more: Could I put it more shortly? Have I said anything that is avoidably ugly?" (Hat tip to the *Economist* style guide for that one.[2])

You might notice that the idea of serving the reader in the realm of writing isn't unlike how the best content marketing serves the customer (or user, a word I hate to use to refer to people).

Yet often in writing and in business we put ourselves first. Many writers, too, think sometimes that it's all about them. And many organizations—especially those with multiple points of review or layers

44

of bureaucracy—tend to place other agendas above the interests of the reader. They hold a spot at the front of the line for the boss, the CEO, the exec, the legal department, whatever . . .

But that's a mistake, because *you* (as a marketer or content creator) should be the customer advocate. The only people your content needs to please are your readers. Because ultimately you serve them, and not your boss or your CEO or your client.

Why? If the customer loves your content, so will your boss or client. But the inverse isn't necessarily true: if only your boss loves it, it won't achieve what your organization needs it to.

So create every bit of content to please just one person: your customer or prospect—*not* your boss (or client, if you're at an agency). Think of it this way: what would your content look like if your customer signed your paycheck? It's up to you to advocate for this point of view.

Relentlessly, unremittingly, obstinately focus on the reader.

So write your first draft as you usually would—then go back and rework it, swapping places with your readers to consider things from their point of view, with honest empathy for the experience you are giving them. Ask yourself:

- ♦ What experience is this creating for the reader?
- ♦ What questions might they have?
- ♦ Am I making them work too hard to figure out what I am trying to say?

11

Humor Comes on the Rewrite

Humor comes on the rewrite. So do the best analogies, the clearest construction, the best writing—period.

I'm breaking this out as a separate rule for emphasis, because reworking the work is what separates us from the chimps. Or at least from self-indulgent writers who put their own needs above their audience's.

12

Develop Pathological Empathy

Some people are naturally empathic. They easily understand another's point of view, and they immediately grok what another might be feeling in any scenario. If that is you, congrats: you're ahead of the game. The rest of us have to work a little harder, and a little more intentionally, to get into the customer mind-set.

"Good writing (and therefore crafting good experiences) requires us to understand and have empathy for our audience, their situation, their needs and goals," says Jonathon Colman of Facebook. "The best content experiences are pitched perfectly in the sweet spot, the nexus of all those human factors."

In other words, empathy for the customer experience should be at the root of all of your content, because having a sense of the people you are writing for and a deep understanding of their problems is key to honing your skill. Content created merely to further a search engine ranking is a waste of time and effort. What matters now is creating useful content that solves customer problems, shoulders their burdens, eases their pain, enriches their lives. We wrote that in *Content Rules*, but recent and various Google updates have seemed to finally make it permanent and official. (Sing hallelujah!)

That means you have to meet people where they are, with an attitude of benevolence and largesse, to help them find answers to the problems they have. All of your content—your product pages, your landing pages, your customer support text, your About Us pages, and so on "need to use language to support people's needs and goals," Colman told me. "And each of those experiences requires very thoughtful writing that's appropriate to what the audience needs from us in those situations. A listicle of 14 Cats Who Look Just Like Elvis just ain't gonna work when someone needs to figure out how our products work."

So how do you know what people need? That's where enormous, mammoth, almost *pathological* empathy comes in. Start by getting to know your customers.

"It's hard to have real empathy for real people's experiences if we don't really get to know the people themselves," Colman said. "Not just in aggregate, not just as a collection of Web analytics data, search queries, or spreadsheets . . . I mean the real deal: actually talking with them. Or, better still: listening to them."

Empathy—like writing—isn't a gift. It's a discipline. It takes some intentional effort and diligence to develop enormous empathy so that you can apply it to your writing. "You're not engaging in a one-time action," Colman says. "You're building a long-term relationship."

Here are some first steps toward building enormous empathy, from Jonathon Colman (the quoted portions are his words from an interview I conducted with him):

1. *Spend time with your customers or prospects.* Spending time with your customers sounds obvious, doesn't it? But it's surprising how few marketers actually interact with their customers; often, only customer service or sales teams do. Listen to customer service inquiries. Watch how customers behave. See what problems they have. "Look for patterns."

2. *Understand their habitat.* "Beyond putting together a focus group in an artificial setting or doing so-called user experience testing in a lab environment, *arrange to visit the people who use your content or products in their natural habitat.* . . . Talk with them in their homes, at their jobs; watch them as they browse your site or use your app on mobile while waiting in line at the coffee shop. This will give you an entirely new understanding of what people need from you and your content. You can't develop empathy without context."

3. *Be a natural skeptic.* A powerful question is, Why? Why do you do things that way? Why do you feel that way?

4. *Ask why they do it.* "Never assume that you know the answer to why your readers or the people who use your products do what

they do . . . You might be great at using analytics systems to measure every nuance of a person's behavior on your site or in your app. But analytics only tell us what people did, not why they did it. So ask. And then ask again. And keep asking until you understand the bigger picture of what people value and what they need from you."

5. *Share story, not just stats.* "A lot of companies build dashboards and monitors that they install all over the office that are filled with analytics data: How many concurrent users are on the site, the data throughput of the app, the number of transactions per hour, and so on."

   But what about feedback from the people on your site or the people using your products? You can display that, too. And while you can build aggregate metrics around this feedback (sentiment, length, complaints per hour, etc.), it's even more powerful to display people's actual comments. Follow that up by building rapid workflows to solve problems and you're putting empathy into action!

I'd add a simple shortcut—an *empathy hack*—to help you get into the customer mind-set:

6. *Use a customer-centric POV.* Replace *I* or *we* with *you* to shift the focus to the customer's point of view. Then write (or rewrite) accordingly. For example:

   Company-centric: *We offer accelerated application development.*

   Customer-centric: *Deploy an app to the cloud at lunch hour. And still have time to eat. (From the home page of Kinvey .com.)*

   Company-centric: *We are the leading global B2B research and advisory firm. We deliver actionable intelligence, strategic and operational frameworks and personal guidance from experienced practitioners. (From Sirius Decisions.[1])*

   Customer-centric: *Make better business decisions based on actionable insight and years of experience placed at your disposal.*

Enormous empathy is especially important for sales copy or marketing landing pages, where you should be very specific about what your value offers *to your customers*—and not just what the offer is, Nadia Eghbal, co-owner of Feast, an online cooking school, told me in an interview.

"Your customers don't buy your product to do your company a favor," Eghbal said. "They're doing it because your product makes their lives better. So if you want to sell something, you need to explain how you're helping them."

On its home page, Feast shifted from company-centric to customer-centric writing, like this:

Company-centric: *A Better Way to Learn How to Cook.* (This statement was too nonspecific, Nadia said. Better in what way? And according to whom?)

Customer-centric: *Become a Cook in 30 Days.*

Eghbal credits Feast's shift in messaging for a tenfold increase in sales, and she cites soul-filling anecdotal evidence, too (actual feedback, as Jonathon Colman advises). "We regularly get emails from people along the lines of 'Wow, everything on your home page describes me to a T!'—which suggests we're resonating with customers in the right way," she said.

And more broadly: the best way to keep readers reading is to talk about them, not you.

13

'Cross Out the Wrong Words'

"Writing is easy," said Mark Twain. "All you have to do is cross out the wrong words."

Revisiting a first draft to rework and rewrite it doesn't sound like much fun, does it? It sounds like drudgery and tedium, like alphabetizing canned goods.

But it's not really, because there's a kind of freedom in it. You've already done the hard part of setting down the words. Now comes the easier (and, for some, less anxiety-inducing) part of distilling it to its essence—or, crossing out the wrong words and the unnecessary words, and sometimes finding better ones to use.

Revising is my favorite part of writing—because it's when I (or you!) do the creative, fun part of writing. To me the first draft feels more like pure ball-and-chain drudgery. The editing is where you get to make some merry.

I'm not talking here about having someone else edit your work, by the way. That comes later. First, you need to take a first pass at shaping your own work—essentially rewriting much of it.

There are two approaches to self-editing:

1. *Developmental editing,* which I call editing by chainsaw. Here's where you look at the big picture.
2. *Line editing,* which I call editing by surgical tools. Here's where you look at paragraph and sentence flow, word choice, usage, and so on.

I like to use both on the same piece, first one . . . and then the other.

Editing by chainsaw. First, ignore the grammar and specific words you've used, and focus on the bigger stuff.

- State your key idea as clearly as you can near the start. You might've gotten bogged down by setting up an idea with too much introductory explanation, instead of just getting right into it. (See Rule 15.) If so, remove that introductory text, whittle it down, or (if it's really good) use it elsewhere.
- Slash anything that feels extraneous—if it doesn't support your main point or further your argument, or if it distracts from the key point. (Even if it's a good story or anecdote.)
- Make every paragraph earn its keep. Does every paragraph contain an idea that the one before or after it doesn't? It should. Are the paragraphs more like Frankenparagraphs—made up of disconnected sentences bolted awkwardly together, creating an ugly mess? They shouldn't be. The sentences should instead build on one another, furthering a single idea and creating a whole.
- Make every sentence earn its keep. Does it bring something unique to the paragraph? Or does it simply restate what its buddy before it already said? If so, kill it. Be ruthless. Adopt a less-is-more mind-set: many writers take too long to get to the point; they use too many words. Don't be that guy. Write concisely.
- Move things around. Are things in the right order? Does one point flow into the next?
- Think of the sentences in a paragraph as a conversation between an elderly, companionable couple. They don't talk over each other; they expand or elucidate what the other before them said.

Editing with surgical tools. Next, turn off the chainsaw and turn back to the words.

- Trim the bloat and fat. Are you ~~potentially~~ using ~~far~~ too many words to say things that might be said ~~more~~ concisely?

- Shed the obvious. There's no need to include *in this article, in this post, in regard to, I've always felt that, we are of the opinion that* . . . You get the idea.
- Lose Frankenwords, word additives, clichés, and words pretending to be something they're not. (See Rules 29 and 30.)
- Trim word bloat. Sub in single words for phrases (some samples: sub *although* for *despite the fact that*; *when* or *in* for *when it comes to*; *when* or *at times* for *there will be times when*; *remains* for *continues to be*; and *about* or *regarding* for *in regard to*).
- Ditch adverbs unless they are necessary to adjust the meaning. (Rule 34.)
- Ditch weakling verbs in favor of stronger, ripped ones. (Rule 33.)
- Create transitions between paragraphs. Good transitions greatly improve the feel and reader-friendliness of any work. The best writing flows from paragraph to paragraph, creating progression and cadence. Good transitions are like fine stitching, turning disconnected writing into a seamless whole.
- Draw natural connections between paragraphs. Again, don't merely rely on high school transitions like *however, thus, therefore*, and so on. Instead, pick up an idea from the previous paragraph and connect it to an idea in the next paragraph.

Did you notice that I just wrote 700 words on editing but didn't once mention grammar? That's not because grammar isn't important. It is, as we'll talk about in Part II. But writers tend to equate editing with fixing the grammar, when it's so much more than that.

Fixing the grammar is copyediting (also important), but it's more important to get the writing right first. You can then go get some help with the copyedit (see Rule 24).

14

Start with *Dear Mom . . .*

What if you have trouble simply getting off the starting block? The fear of the blank page is the number one cliché in writing. "Some call it writer's block. Others call it procrastination," photographer and author Dane Sanders told me. Whatever you call it, it stops people from writing even before they start.

I don't believe in writer's block. "My father never got truck driver's block," as the journalist Roger Simon has said.[1] A house framer isn't daunted by the pile of two-by-fours. Nor was Edison intimidated by the blank lightbulb, points out Colin Nissan in a piece on the humor website McSweeney's.[2]

More often than not, writer's block—or the reluctance to begin—is rooted in fear and anxiety about knowing where, exactly, to start. I get that, because I procrastinate, too.

Before I begin to write, I pay all my bills. I catch up on any movies or TV series I might've never gotten around to seeing. I change the oil in my car. I waste an hour or two on Facebook. I descale the coffee maker. I decide to create something really complicated for dinner. Only then do I leash up my dog and decide on the walk what the first line I'm going to write will be when I get back home.

So I might not believe in writer's block, but I do believe in writer's evasion. I believe in writer's difficulty and writer's procrastination and writer's I-wonder-if-there's-any-donuts-left?-I-should-go-check.

A writing GPS can certainly help lubricate the start, as we've discussed. But at some point you just have to start writing.

In a piece in the *New Yorker*, John McPhee suggests the trick of typing *Dear Mother* to neuter the fear of the blank page.[3] You could do that, or adapt it to *Dear Dad, Hi hon,* or *Hey you.*

If you're a marketing or business writer, you can adapt that approach by thinking of your favorite customer—and not some nameless, faceless market segment. Keep a real person you either know or you can imagine knowing in mind. Someone you like, too, because you want to help this person.

McPhee's trick is also handy to use as a general approach, because it requires you to picture the reader on the receiving end of your writing as someone you know personally. Doing that helps relax your writing voice into sounding natural and loose and accessible.

In other words, by framing your writing as a conversation with someone specific, you become more . . . well, conversational.

15

If You Take a Running Start, Cover Your Tracks

At the beginning of a piece, many of us take too long to delve into the topic. We offer too much setup and background. In other words, we take a metaphorical running start on the page—before getting to the real starting point.

It's a great way to warm up to a topic, and I do it all the time. But in most cases I go back and erase the running start, covering my tracks completely and getting to the key point more directly.

One of my professors in college used to routinely lop off the first paragraph or two from our essays. Usually that barely affected the meaning—but greatly improved that first impression I talk about elsewhere here.

Try it with the next piece you write: Can you trim the start, or lop it off completely? Does doing that help the reader get into the heart of things more quickly?

Take a look at an example from MarketingProfs. Here are the unedited first few paragraphs of a submission we received recently about using YouTube to market a business:

> *Simultaneous to the modern boom of Web 2.0 and along with the rise of social media, companies have projected their presence by utilizing social media giants (e.g., Facebook and Twitter) in attempts to market their businesses.*

And while companies have seen much success in tapping the vein of reaching the masses through the few quintessential social networks, only a fraction have explored the option of YouTube marketing.

Let's take a look at the facts.

YouTube is not only the second largest search engine, but also the third most visited website in the world, only behind Google and Facebook. It receives over 1 billion unique monthly visitors and has about 6 billion hours of videos watched each month. Let that sink in.

Almost that entire first paragraph can be sliced off the top without losing much context. Doing so gets into the point of the piece more quickly and clearly, and with brevity. This is the same piece, post-editing:

Though many companies have succeeded in reaching their audiences via social networks such as Facebook and Twitter, only a fraction have explored the option of marketing via YouTube.

Yet, YouTube is not only the second-largest search engine but also the third most-visited website in the world, only behind Google and Facebook. It receives over 1 billion unique monthly visitors, and it has about 6 billion hours of videos watched each month.

Let those numbers sink in for a minute . . .

And here's another from Salon. These are the first two paragraphs of an article that ran Memorial Day weekend in 2014:

With Memorial Day weekend, we finally have the traditional, though not technical, beginning of summer. (Given 2014 weather patterns, however, we will probably get at least 10 more Weather Channel-christened "Snowstorm Frodo" blizzards by July 4. How about that weather, eh?) But anyway. Memorial Day weekend is another great opportunity for the whole family to gather at a beach house or, if traffic's unmanageable, a makeshift interstate-median campsite. Or maybe you will be alone? Don't feel bad. Being alone during one of the year's most fun three-day weekends can be . . . good?

So, you're at the barbecue, or the fake Disneyland picnic table, and everyone's having a good time noshing on cheeseburgers or chicken things or other meats or quinoa. Uncle Dingo's talking about his kids' (your cousins') mediocre peewee baseball performance this spring, and then that leads to discussion of the current Major League Baseball standings, maybe that leads to some light chatter about the weather, the accuracy of Thomas Piketty's data integration, the price of beans, etc. And then right when Cousin Tombert, who just graduated college with a B.A. in medieval poetry gender roles and is about to start a job leading the complex derivative trading desk at a Greenwich-based hedge fund, is walking out with Cool Whip and those poor-man's strawberry shortcake shells that the grocery stores sell in six-packs, Uncle Dingo, out of nowhere, goes, ". . . well, what do you expect, in a world where President Hussein Obama thinks he doesn't need Congress anymore.[1]

Author Jim Newell is a good writer—and the style of the piece is breezy, intentionally meandering, and funny. But still Jim could've easily lopped off that first paragraph for a quicker start.

16

Notice Where Words Appear in Relation to Others around Them

Misplaced modifiers and odd word order are among the most common errors I see made by marketers—and by most writers, for that matter. They are also the easiest to correct.

Here's an example (adapted from a Chyten workbook exercise) of a misplaced modifier (in this case, also called a dangling modifier):

Original: We thought the New York Yankees sucked, having just returned from the play-off game.

Corrected: Having just returned from the play-off game, we thought the New York Yankees sucked.

Or even better: We saw the New York Yankees in the play-off game and thought they sucked.

Why? Because *we*—not the Yankees—returned from the game and we thought they sucked.

Here's another example:

Original: Though often misunderstood, scholars know that anarchy does not mean chaos.

Corrected: Though often misunderstood, anarchy does not mean chaos, as scholars well know.

What's misunderstood is the term *anarchy*, not the scholars (though they, too, are often misunderstood—all the more reason not to dangle that modifying phrase).

Once you start paying attention to misplaced modifiers and confusing word order, you'll notice it everywhere. One word you'll see frequently misplaced is *only*.

So it's not: Only publish good content.

It's actually: Publish only good content.

Why? Because the idea isn't that you should only publish—and not, say, also create and distribute—good content; the idea is that the content you publish should be good.

In other words, *only* needs to modify *good content*, not *publish*. (A handy writing hack is to think twice about placing *only* immediately before a verb.)

17

'A Good Lede Invites You to the Party and a Good Kicker Makes You Wish You Could Stay Longer'

Give special love to the first and last sentences of your piece—the opening and closing, or the *lede* (*lead*)[1] and *kicker*—in traditional journalism terms. Why do that? As Articulate Marketing's Matthew Stibbe explains, "A good lede invites you to the party and a good kicker makes you wish you could stay longer."[2] This rule honors him.

A good lead, then, sets the tone for your writing and hooks the reader into wanting to know more. Here are some options:

- ◆ **Put your reader into the story.** Put your reader—or someone just like your reader—into the story. You might share an anecdote about someone grappling with a problem your piece solves, or set up a scenario your reader will recognize. For example, consider this lede to a MarketingProfs article by Ernest Nicastro, on what marketers can learn from Abraham Lincoln's Gettysburg Address:

  > It is a crisp, clear autumn afternoon, about 1:30. A full sun hangs in a bright blue sky. A large crowd mills about.
  >
  > Imagine that you are there. You jostle for position. You strain your neck to get a glimpse. You cup your hand behind your ear . . . as the 16th President of the United States steps to the center of the platform and begins his "few appropriate remarks."[3]

61

♦ **Describe a problem your reader can relate to.** This lead from online publication Thrillist puts readers in a place they can identify with:

> *You're on vacation, dammit, and ready to let loose. Check out a museum? Ogle architecture? No thanks. Because you know that true cultural immersion begins (and ends) at a watering hole or epic party, where you can rub shoulders with local drunks.*[4]

♦ **Set a stage.** This is from Demian Farnworth, writing at the website Copyblogger, setting a stage in his lead to "13 Damn Good Ideas from 13 Dead Copywriters":[5]

> *Advertising is an ancient art.*
>
> *In the Babylonian sea ports, merchants hired barkers to announce the arrival of wine, spices, and fabrics.*
>
> *Citizens in Greece hung "Lost" posters in hopes of being reunited with children, jewelry, or slaves.*
>
> *And elaborately painted signs (billboards) sprung up throughout Pompeii to announce plays, carnivals, and races.*
>
> *Surprised?*
>
> *You shouldn't be. The history of advertising is full of the tools, tactics, and strategies you—as online marketer—still use.*
>
> *Let me show you why this matters.*

♦ **Ask a question.** Upworthy.com offers a good example of starting a piece by asking a question in "This School Struggled with Detentions, so They Asked for Students' Help":[6]

> *What if there were a simple and cheap way to keep kids out of detention and from eventually heading down the wrong path? This school seems to have figured it out, and it's kinda genius.*

Use this one infrequently, as the technique gets tiresome otherwise. You want to avoid sounding like a one-note, late-night infomercial ("Did you ever wonder . . . ?").

♦ **Quote a crazy or controversial bit of data.** Grounding the lead in a crazy stat that blows your reader away is a way to shock the reader into sitting up a little taller and paying attention, in a *Wait . . . what?* kind of way. Like this, from Fast Company:

> *A recent, widely circulated study found that one-third of Americans who bought a wearable tech product ditched it within six months. So why are companies as diverse as Google, Nike, Pepsi, and Disney pumping plenty of cash—and new life—into the technology?*[7]

◆ **Tell a story or relay a personal anecdote.** The *New Yorker* does this a lot. Here's the lead from a piece by Richard Brody:

> *My artistic career was ended by Godzilla—as a child monster-movie maniac, I stopped attending painting classes when the long-awaited film . . . showed up on Saturday-morning television . . . I missed the 2004 screenings of the restoration, so this revival is a welcome chance to catch up with it, and the experience is surprising.*[8]

Notice how Brody's lead is stronger because he ends it, appropriately enough, with a curiosity-eliciting cliffhanger: In what way was it surprising? How so?

◆ **Other ideas.** You could do other things, too. Start with a quote. Use an analogy. Make a bold statement. Whatever you do, do it up—because your lead sentence or sentences are among the most important words you'll string together.

I'd put closings, or kickers, as a close second in importance to the lead. Finish strong, with a call to action (if appropriate) and a sense of completion, rather than merely trailing off as if you ran out of steam.

You can pose a question or challenge to the reader, of course: so what do you think? That's obvious, and it's also the easy way out. Instead, you might try these techniques:

◆ **Recast the biggest takeaway of the piece.** Try restating the main point of your piece—not as pure regurgitation, of course, but as a kind of synthesized summary.

On AnnHandley.com, that's what I did in a post about how Honey Maid graham crackers dealt with haters in a recent campaign:

Writing at MarketingProfs today, Carla Ciccotelli offers advice for brands dealing with haters, especially in our social media world. My favorite line from her post is this: "When dealing with complaints, think of the bigger picture and the effect public complaints will have on your business.

I love the part about a bigger picture—especially when it helps a company make it clear what it stands for. And also—and this is gutsier—what it clearly won't stand.[9]

♦ **Add an element of tonal surprise.** "Turn the story around," suggests Matthew Stibbe. "If you've been formal, go relaxed. If you're relaxed, become formal." He cites a recent example from *Wired* magazine: "It takes a clean digital signal from your USB port and converts it to a warm analog music. And it looks as badass as it sounds."[10]

♦ **Let others have the last word.** If you've interviewed someone for an article or post, consider ending with a direct quote from that person.

In a post I wrote about quantifying the results of an Instagram campaign by the Toronto Silent Film Festival, I wanted Festival Director Shirley Hughes to have the last word:

We want our audiences to go away from the experience wanting more and realizing that a good story, excellent cinematography, direction and acting to make a good film is what is needed to connect with them. When I have teenage boys come out [from] a screening of the Black Pirate [from] 1925 with Douglas Fairbanks and exclaim "that was the coolest!" you know you are doing the right thing.[11]

18

Show, Don't Tell

"Don't tell me that the moon is shining," wrote Russian playwright and short-story writer Anton Chekhov. "Show me the glint of moon on broken glass."

Show, don't tell is a *Content Rules* rule, and it's also moonlighting here as a writing rule. Good content—and good writing—doesn't preach or hard-sell. Instead, it shows how your product or service lives in the world, explaining in human terms how it adds value to people's lives, eases troubles, shoulders burdens, and meets needs.

I like how Aaron Orendorff frames the idea of showing, not telling. Think about it as "salvation, not sales. Theology, not transactions," he writes on his site, IconicContent.com.

"Ask yourself, 'What hell does my product save people *from*? And what heaven does it *deliver them unto*?'" Aaron explains.

The idea is entirely secular, of course. "There are lots of hells and good marketing takes advantage of them all the time," Aaron says. "There's no-time hell, stressed-out hell, bored hell, out-of-shape hell, lonely hell, overworked hell, no-budget hell, debt hell, bad-hygiene hell, low-CTR [click-through rate] hell, human-relations hell, disorganized hell . . . you get the idea."[1]

In other words, don't talk about your features, benefits, and shining moons. Tell me—better yet, show me—why they matter *to me*.

And how do you do that?

Details are what make your words come alive. You'd think the generic and nonspecific might apply broadly—and therefore almost anyone reading the description of a product or service would come to regard it as being relevant to them.

But the truth is that specific details make content vibrant, and they add a necessary human element that makes your content more relatable. Details paint a fuller, clearer, picture and give readers necessary footholds for getting more involved or vested in the writing.

(That brings to mind a gem from my journalism school days: Be specific enough to be believable, but universal enough to be credible.)

Natalie Goldberg describes the practice of adding details as giving things "the dignity of their names."

"Just as with human beings, it is rude to say, 'Hey, girl, get in line.'" she writes in her book on writing, *Writing Down the Bones*.[2] "That 'girl' has a name."

So, whenever possible, specify *geranium* instead of *flower*, as Natalie suggests. Or substitute *cocker spaniel* for *dog*. Or write *Vietnamese sandwich truck* instead of *food-truck service*. Or *Alan Arakelian from Accounting* instead of *client*.

Especially in a business-to-business scenario, specific details can help put flesh and blood on the dry bones of a so-called solution, making it real and palpable to the people you are trying to reach. It's particularly effective in giving personality to case studies and customer testimonials.

For example, if I were Cisco Systems and trying to show how the role of information technology (IT) is changing, I could commission a white paper detailing new consumption models brought about by cloud, security, mobility, and programmable networks. I might talk about how that is creating new markets and business models, transforming communication and knowledge sharing, and significantly changing the role of IT.

Or . . .

I could tell you a story about a real chief information officer who shares in clear, simple language how she's using technology to sell more beer to the people who want to buy it.

Which would you find more compelling? The generic or the specific?

I suppose my setup wasn't entirely fair. The business world has room for both: complex whitepapers that give a comprehensive look at the changing world of IT, and lighter, specific, story-based content that adds a heartbeat and a pulse to an idea. But a story featuring a real person and a real solution to a real problem is a far livelier approach for customer videos and in-person testimonials—as opposed to, say, the canned customer testimonials that businesses tend to trot out.

Cisco in fact did produce a video story and site content that features a CIO—Marina Bellini of Grupo Modelo in Mexico. (Grupo Modelo exports Corona, among other beer brands.)

Cisco's Voice of the Customer team—featuring Tim Washer, Andy Capener, and Chris Huston—created the video, one of three featuring actual CIOs having real conversations about jobs they pretty much love. Here's what any company can take away from that video series in using it as the model for an effective, specific approach:

- **Ban Frankenspeak.** In a lot of customer videos, folks speak in corporate lingo, using buzzwords and talking points. But CIOs are real people with real personalities. I like the innovative approach of showing true personality in corporate IT.

  How did Cisco pull it off? "A key to getting people into a relaxed, conversational state of mind is getting the right environment," Tim told me. "We knew we did *not* want to shoot this in a conference room, but instead wanted to show these folks in some nonbusiness-related setting and interrupt that [reversion to a corporate persona]."

- **Align story and strategy.** Tell a specific, simple story really well, aligned with a bigger idea and broader strategy. We're all familiar with the classic voice-of-the-customer talking-head video. Rather than using the typical corporate approach, Cisco sought to create a different model.

"We wanted to add an entertainment element, which I think is critical for a video to find an audience on YouTube," Tim said. They also wanted to humanize the companies—both Cisco and the client company—by letting the audience see a personable, conversational side of both.

(Notice how I said *personable*, not *personal?* The CIOs aren't talking about their home lives or children or pets; the video isn't personal. But they do talk about business with plenty of personality. That's personable—and to my mind a sweet spot for business-to-business companies.)

As for the bigger strategy? That was to highlight how modern CIOs think more strategically, transforming IT from a cost center to a revenue center—by connecting to new customers and new markets.

Of course, the key to all of this—making words come alive, adding a human element, and being personable and compelling—is to be specific. To show, not merely tell.

19

Use Familiar Yet Surprising Analogies

An analogy is a comparison that frames the unknown with the known. Think of an analogy as a kind of gift to your readers that helps explain a complex process or concept with familiar, relatable specifics. In other words, it helps make the abstract more concrete.

Remember the example from Rule 5 that referenced the literacy stat?

"According to the National Assessment of Adult Literacy (NAAL), released in 2006 by the U.S. Department of Education, 30 million adults struggle with basic reading tasks."

Thirty million sounds like a lot. But is it? It's about 12 percent of the population (that helps) or just over the total population of Texas (much better).

You could say you've acquired 842 new accounts in 2014. Or you could put that into context by pointing out that it's more than the capacity of the London Eye.

I like the way the *Guardian* used familiar but surprising analogies in a piece to explain why NSA (National Security Agency) access and privacy should freak us all out.

"You don't need to be talking to a terror suspect to have your communication data analysed by the NSA," the *Guardian* wrote, because the agency is allowed to travel three hops (degrees of separation) from its targets—"who could be people who talk to people who talk to people who talk to you."[1]

So if you have 200 friends on Facebook (just over the average number of friends there), three hops gives the NSA access to a network that exceeds the population of Minnesota.

Of course, your audience should be familiar with the elements of your analogy. (Yet another reason to know your audience.) You might have arcane and specific knowledge of, say, the topography of Karabakh or Kosovo. But does your audience?

At the same time, the best analogies have an element of surprise to them, and they don't rely on obvious clichés (e.g., *as big as four football fields*).

For example, instead of describing something as *huge*, provide a familiar but interesting context:

> *Instead of:* The leaves of the giant pumpkin plant are huge.
>
> *Try:* The pumpkin leaves are the size of trash-can lids, covering pumpkins the size of beer kegs.
>
> *Instead of:* The pavement is covered with tiny speed bumps that are 10–12 millimeters in diameter.
>
> *Try:* The pavement is covered with tiny speed bumps that are about as large as a quarter.
>
> *Better still:* The pavement is covered with tiny speed bumps that look like acorn caps under the tar.

Ground your data or your text in the familiar yet the surprising, taking it out of the theoretical and into the real and visceral.

20

Approach Writing Like Teaching

Good, *pathologically* empathic writing strives to explain, to make things a little bit clearer, to make sense of our world—even if it's just a straightforward product description.

"A writer always tries . . . to be part of the solution, to understand a little about life and to pass this on," says the writer Anne Lamott.[1]

It's easy to embrace the teaching mind-set when you're writing a how-to or other bit of instruction. But the notion is broader than that: strive to explain your point of view to your reader with supporting evidence and context.

Don't just tell your readers that you feel something; tell them *why* you feel it. Don't just say what works; tell them *why* it works and what led you to this moment.

Be as specific as possible:

- Don't say *solution*—tell me what your product does.
- Don't say *a lot*—tell me how many.

Keep it *simple*—but not simplistic (see Rule 21).

21

Keep It Simple—but Not Simplistic

Any fool can make something complicated. It takes a genius to make it simple.

—Woody Guthrie

Business—like life—can be complicated. Products can be intricate and concepts may seem impenetrable. But good content deconstructs the complex to make it easily understood: It sheds the corporate Frankenspeak. It conveys things in concise, human, accessible terms.

A bit of wisdom from my journalism days: *No one will ever complain that you've made things too simple to understand.* Of course, *simple* does not equal *dumbed down.* Another gem from my journalism professors: *Assume the reader knows nothing. But don't assume the reader is stupid.*

If you think your business-to-business concept is too complex to be conveyed simply, take a look at the very first line of the *Economist*'s style guide (www.economist.com/styleguide/introduction): "The first requirement of *The Economist* is that it should be readily understandable. Clarity of writing usually follows clarity of thought. So think what you want to say, then say it as simply as possible."

Here's where the marketing department can really help add value in a business context, because *simple* means *making it easy for the customer.* It means being the customer's advocate. As Boston-based content strategist Georgy Cohen writes (in the context of creating website content), "The marketer should be identifying (and ruthlessly refining) the core messages and the top goals, then working with the Web professionals to create a website supporting them."[1]

Simplicity comes primarily from approaching any writing with empathy and a reader-centric point of view to begin with—that is, it's the result of writing with clarity and brevity, and in human language, as we've been talking about here. But also consider the vehicle carrying the message: Maybe you don't need words at all. Or maybe you need a cleaner, simpler look for the words you do use. Think about these:

- ◆ **Finding the best fit for your message.** Do we need more or fewer words? Would a chart or graphic or visual convey an idea more simply? Would a video convey what we are trying to say more directly?

- ◆ **Designing with your words, rather than fitting words into a design.** This isn't a book on design, of course. Nonetheless, the visual treatment of words on a page (digital or actual) can greatly enhance their effectiveness. So here are two things to keep in mind:

  1. *White space is a prerequisite, not a luxury.* Large chunks of text are formidable and depressing. Designers will tell you that more white space makes your work readable, and it's true. It also gives your words oxygen, allowing them to breathe and live on the page with plenty of room to relax—instead of being jumbled together in a kind of content shantytown or ghetto.

  2. *Make your words the hero of your design,* rather than adding them to a completed design the way a supermarket baker pipes a name into the blank field on a prebaked birthday cake from the case. Pasting words into a blank space without respecting their role in a design is called the *lorem ipsum* approach, a name that refers to the nonsense Latin text that printers and typesetters have used since the 1500s as placeholder (or dummy) text. That approach treats the content as secondary to the design.

     For a marketer, design and content aren't separate processes; they are actually key parts of the same process. They are best friends and life partners, and they deserve to be treated as such.

22

Find a Writing Buddy

If writing were a sport, it would be a tennis match played against a brick wall, or a solo game of tetherball. You can do it, but it's a little lonely.

Finding a writing buddy can feel like having someone to train and volley with. Together you might brainstorm ideas, give new writing a first read, give feedback, suggest improvements . . . in short, prod each other to do better work. A writing buddy is someone who's in your corner.

Friends and colleagues can certainly play that role if you share a similar sensibility. Or you can connect with like-minded writers online. You can find and connect with other writers in countless online forums, LinkedIn communities, and Google and Facebook groups to share resources and ideas. Most of them have a literary bent.

Here are some with member bases that are either made up of generalists or nonfiction writers:

- ♦ LinkEds and Writers (LinkedIn.com) calls itself the "biggest and best LinkedIn group for editors, proofreaders and writers." It's a private group. Once you're approved, you'll find it a rich resource for writing advice, support, and tips.
- ♦ *Copyblogger*'s forums (copyblogger.com) consist of various specific and general subgroups.
- ♦ Co-writers.com (co-writers.com) is where you can find collaboration partners or sources for stories.

- The Writer's Digest forum (writersdigest.com/forum) is geared mostly toward literary writers, but there is a specific forum for writers seeking buddies.
- National Novel Writing Month (nanowrimo.org) is a nonprofit that promotes a seat-of-your-pants approach to creative writing each November, when aspiring novelists commit to writing a 50,000-word novel by the stroke of midnight on the last day of the month. Year-round, the site offers resources for writers, including a Critique, Feedback & Novel Swaps Forum. Again, it's more of a literary site, but it has some utility for nonfiction writers.
- MarketingProfs Content Marketing Crash Course and Content Marketing Bootcamp Facebook groups are exclusive to members of the MarketingProfs University content and writing courses; they are a great place to network with instructors and students.

23

Avoid Writing by Committee

Having a buddy by your side is helpful. Having an entire committee on your back? Not so much.

Writing is often like parenting: Everyone believes they know how to do it effectively (especially those who don't have children). If your writing is subject to committee or client approvals, here's some advice on how to neuter the know-it-alls and mean-wells:

- Get sign-off on the bones of the outline, *then* start writing. (You can often avoid a lot of angst this way.)
- Set clear expectations for how many rounds are acceptable in the approval process. One is fine. Five? Nope.
- Seek an OK, not opinions. *Please approve* is likely to deliver far fewer edits than will *please tell me if you have suggestions.*

24

Hire a Great Editor

Writers have their name on a work, so they naturally get a lot of credit. But behind the scenes, a good editor adds a lot to the process.

Remember what I said previously, about the two kinds of people? Those who think they can write, and those who think they can't? And very often both are wrong? A good editor teases the best out of self-described writers and nonwriters alike.

The best writing—like the best parts of life, perhaps—is collaborative. It needs a great editor.

There are three major types of editors:

1. Copyeditors/proofreaders, who check facts and wield a push broom to clean up messy style issues, punctuation, typos, misspelling, and so on.
2. Substantive editors, who give a piece of writing a higher level read and offer suggestions on how parts of it might be improved or which parts need to be expanded or condensed. Their review includes broad feedback on things like the overall development of a piece.
3. Line editors, who comb through a piece to correct grammar, word choice, and paragraph and sentence flow—while doing a good deal of rewriting as well, all without overwhelming a writer's voice.

The first type is relatively easy to find (see Part VI: Content Tools); the second, less so; and the third, less still . . . because editing is a nuanced, collaborative approach that can be specific to a writer. I've worked with many, many editors over my career, and in my experience great line editors are hard to find. If you find one, hold on to him or her; get married, if you must.

And then when your friends ask whether you know a good editor, don't give up the name. Simply shrug and change the subject.

25

Be Rabid about Readability

I n this book I advocate using a general approach to creating content that's more relaxed and less filled with jargon, buzzwords, and clichés. In general, the best Web writing isn't necessarily short, but it is simple, with . . .

- shorter paragraphs with no more than three sentences or six lines (and just one is fine).
- shorter sentences with no more than 25 words in a sentence.
- straightforward words—in other words, avoid clichés, jargon, and buzzwords (for example, avoid *utilize* when you can write *use*, instead).

So . . .

- Use bulleted or numbered lists.
- *Highlight key points* (like this one), either in bold or italic, or as a pull quote.
- Use subheadings to break up text.
- Add visual elements, such as graphics, photos, slide shows, and so on.
- Use lots of white space to give your text room to breathe.

But obviously these are only guidelines; I can't know your precise situation. For example, sometimes jargon might be necessary—if you are writing for the technology or medical markets, say. The best advice, as always, is to know your audience.

Some writing experts suggest you check the readability score of your text to ensure that it isn't too difficult for the Web reader. *Difficult* doesn't mean you have an audience full of village idiots; it simply recognizes that in most cases reading online text is different from reading print. Online we tend to scan more, so shorter words and sentences become even more important.

There are several readability scoring methods, but the best known is Flesch-Kincaid, in part because it's embedded in Microsoft Word. It's also embedded in some WordPress plug-ins, including Yoast's search engine optimization plug-in.

Before I go on: a confession. I have a bit of love-hate for readability scoring methodologies, in part because I think writers should rely on their own sensibilities to determine whether their writing is on target for their audiences. In other words, relying on a formula to spit out a score seems like you're selling yourself short.

On the other hand, readability scores can be useful if you're facing a steep learning curve in getting to know a new audience. And I get that you sometimes might need a little extra data to convince a boss or client that something is on target. Plus, readability tests can be kind of fun to use.

So I'm including them here. And I'll quit being judgy about their use.

The Flesch-Kincaid method was developed by Austrian-born Rudolf Flesch, who fled to the United States to avoid the Nazi invasion. He studied law in his home country before going on to graduate from Columbia University with a PhD in English. Flesch was also a writing consultant and the co-creator, with J. Peter Kincaid, of the Flesch-Kincaid readability test, which they developed in 1975 under contract to the U.S. Navy.

Flesch, who died in 1986, was a huge proponent of writing in plain English, championing the use of colloquial and informal words, and authoring several books arguing for plain English, including the classic *The Art of Plain Talk* (published in 1946) and *How to Write Plain English: A Book for Lawyers and Consumers* (published in 1979), the latter of which he produced while working as a communication and writing consultant to the Federal Trade Commission.

But anyway, Flesch said his formula for readability is based on the way the human mind works.

When any of us is reading, the mind and eyes focus on *successive points*, allowing for a tentative judgment to be made about what the text means up to that point. Natural breaks in the text—such as punctuation marks or new paragraphs—allow the mind to reevaluate the text up to that point, because the mind stops for a split second, until it eventually arrives at the final meaning.

So, the longer the word, sentence, or paragraph, the longer the brain has to postpone comprehending ideas until it can reach a point where all of the words, together, make sense.

Because they require more mental work by the reader, longer words and sentences are harder to read and understand.

Writing in MarketingProfs, Grant Draper of the United Kingdom's Vibe Tech Media explains how you can figure out the Flesch-Kincaid score of a piece of your writing manually. (The math-inclined can check out Draper's article at bit.ly/MarketingReadability.)

The higher the score, the easier the piece is to understand. So if its readability score is . . .

90.0–100.0, it is easily understood by an average 11-year-old student

60.0–70.0, it is easily understood by students 13–15 years old

0.0–30.0, it is best understood by university graduates

Flesch recommended that the score of an average, nontechnical piece aimed at consumers be a minimum of 80 (or approximately 15 words per sentence and between 1 and 1.5 syllables per word). For much marketing content, a score of 60 or above works.

Here are some examples of average scores for various types of content using the Flesch-Kincaid scale:

- Comics: 92
- Consumer ads: 82
- *Reader's Digest*: 65
- *Time* magazine: 52
- *Harvard Business Review*: 43
- Standard insurance policy: 10

Microsoft Office products include a readability scoring tool based on the Flesch-Kincaid formula. It looks different on a Mac versus a PC, but here's how to enable it on a PC, as explained by Microsoft:[1]

1. Click the *Microsoft Office* button (at the top left of the page). Click the *File* tab, then click *Options* (at the very bottom of the dialog box).
2. Click *Proofing*.
3. Make sure the *Check grammar with spelling* check box is selected.
4. Under *When correcting spelling and grammar in Word*, select the *Show readability statistics* check box.

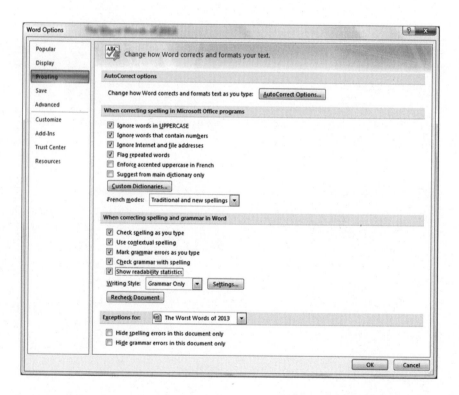

Check the document for spelling and grammar, and you'll see a box displaying statistics and scores.

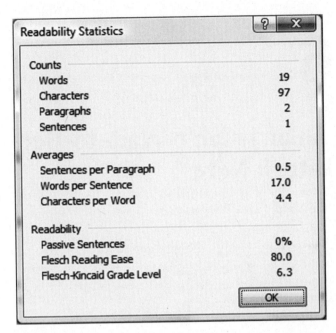

If you've finished your post only to find it's readable only by academics and eggheads, try fixing the basics. Break up long sentences into smaller sentences. Cut out complex words. Simplify. In his day, Flesch maintained that there are no complex, legalistic words and phrases that can't be translated into plain English. (Remember, he was the guy who wrote the book on simple language for lawyers!)

Here are some other quick and easy options for checking readability:

- Read-able (http://read-able.com)
- Editcentral (limited to 50,000 characters at a time; www.editcentral .com/gwt1/EditCentral.html#style_diction)
- Readability Formulas (limited to 600 words at a time, but runs your content through seven formulas; www.readabilityformulas .com/free-readability-formula-tests.php)
- Online-Utility.org (suggests sentences to revise; www.online-utility.org/english/readability_test_and_improve.jsp)

26

End on an I-Can't-Wait-to-Get-Back-to-It Note

It's tempting to push through writing in order to finish a piece by the end of the day, just so you can be done with it and move on. But it can be useful to leave something undone—to give you a reason, and the courage, to start again the next day.

So I like to end a writing session when things are going well and not when I'm sucking wind, so that the next time I pick up that writing again (to rewrite, edit, or whatever) I have some momentum carrying me into it.

Doing so gives me a place to start—which increases the likelihood of an *actual* start, and decreases the likelihood that I'll opt to binge-watch the first three seasons of *Scandal* rather than sitting down at my desk again.

27

Set a Goal Based on Word Count (Not Time)

You can't improve what you don't measure is the old management maxim highlighting data's vital relationship to effectiveness. It's sometimes attributed to Peter Drucker and sometimes to statistician William Edwards Deming (although neither actually said it—but that's a conversation for another day).

In writing, measuring effectiveness might be more nuanced: I'd rather produce 500 awesome words than 10,000 terrible ones, for example. Nonetheless, putting some goals and metrics in place has value for anyone who wants to become a more agile and hale writer.

But make sure you measure your writing in output (words) rather than in effort expended (time). Staring at an empty page for half an hour doesn't count, nor does half an hour of really good thinking, for that matter (at least in this case). In other words (specifically, Yoda's): "There is no try, there is only do."

That approach is especially useful if you are working on a large writing project—such as a white paper, e-book, or video script. What specific number you choose for your daily writing goal is entirely arbitrary; you set your own benchmark.

As I've said, everybody writes: Type an email recently? Submit a report? Respond to a tweet? So if you want to be a writer, you already are. "You're in if you want to be," says writer and photographer Dane Sanders.

Not that long ago, Dane produced two books in the same year for Random House. Both books became best sellers. He'd always made writing a daily habit, he said, but the grind of churning out two books made writing feel like a death march. So he opted out of writing for a while.

Recently, after trying various ways to reignite his routine, he found the most success by simply keeping an appointment with himself, and clocking a daily metric.

The key is knowing your weight class, Dane told me, referring to an idea that he got from marketer and author Mitch Joel:

> *What I mean by it is you need to know whether you're writing with the heavyweights or the featherweights or somewhere in between. If you don't know, no problem, assume it's the featherweights.*
>
> *If heavyweights can churn out 5,000 words in a sitting before breakfast, and you're just beginning your writing routine, make 50 words a win. In many cases, that's about a tweet's worth of content. Most adults I know can do that right now. With that done, up your weight class to say 250 words or 500 words, but keep working until you can get a minimum of 750 words completed in every sitting without too much pain.*

(750 words totals about three pages of text, and in writing circles it seems a kind of magic number traced back to Julia Cameron's notion of morning pages from her book *The Artist's Way*.)

Dane's weight class right now is just north of 1,000 words. My own is about the same. "That means I don't ever feel good about a day unless I have a minimum of at least that many words put together around a single, complete idea," Dale said. "Every time I do that I give myself credit and all is right in my writing world."

When Dane does that for a year, he said, he's produced the equivalent of about 1,500 pages. "I do that two years in a row, and I have a greater word count than Tolstoy's *War and Peace*," which, Dane said, "is not bad for a middleweight."

28

Deadlines Are the WD–40 of Writing

In Pixar's *Toy Story 2*, Woody's kidnapper, Al McWhiggin (the owner of Al's Toy Barn), calls The Cleaner to repair Woody when the toy's arm falls off.

Al asks The Cleaner: "So, uh, how long is this gonna take?" And The Cleaner replies: "You can't rush art." (Which is apparently Pixar's mantra too.)

But forget that mantra. Because at some point, you *do* have to rush your own art. Otherwise, your art sits on its butt on the couch eating chips and salsa.

However many words you write per day, at some point you've got to be done. Really done. With no going back. "Art is never finished, only abandoned," as Leonardo da Vinci said.

I'm an endless tweaker, editor, and tinkerer with my own work. I'm also an excellent procrastinator. And that's the thing about writing—a thing both frustrating and awesome. You can always polish. You can always correct. You can always think of ways you could make it better, or more elegant, or more compelling to read.

But here's the only thing that works for me, and for others like me, including marketer Doug Kessler (of Velocity Partners in the United Kingdom), who originally came up with this rule, "Deadlines *are* the WD-40 of writing."

So give yourself a hard deadline. And then strictly adhere to it. Be stern with yourself: don't allow yourself to float it further out, or treat it as a mere suggestion, or disregard it entirely.

Do the best work you can by the deadline you've set, and then consider your writing project finished.

Part II

Writing Rules: Grammar and Usage

Most people think that writing is grammar. But (as I hope you gleaned from Part I) good writing is more about thinking, rewriting, and keeping your focus relentlessly on the reader than it is about knowing your *affect* from your elbow (and your *effect*, too).

Not that grammar and usage aren't important. They are. But in many ways they are secondary. Which is why this section is . . . well, second.

Grammar and usage are a bit of a rabbit hole. You start talking about word choice and *who* and *whom* and active and passive and the next thing you know you and I are both exhausted and overwhelmed—it seems easier to just give up entirely rather than risk breaking a grammar rule.

So let's not go there. What I've tried to give you here are rules of grammar and usage curated for a marketing audience. They are based on my experience of what issues tend to cause marketers the most trouble, grammarily speaking.

(That is, if grammarily is a word.)

(Which I'm pretty sure it's not.)

29

Use Real Words

Real words seem harder to come by than you might think. The promise of the social Web is in part its ability to reveal the individual people—not markets, or demographic segments, or data sets—that are our customers (and ourselves). That isn't a revolutionary concept: almost 15 years ago, Rick Levine and his colleagues said as much in *The Cluetrain Manifesto*.

William Strunk and E. B. White told their readers in *The Elements of Style*: "Write in a way that comes naturally . . . Prefer the standard to the offbeat."[1] In other words, write for real people, using real words.

Yet here we are, decades later, and our writing and content are still littered with revolutionary, value-added, impactful, cutting-edge, best-of-breed, go-to ideated words designed to leverage and incentivize and synergize the current paradigm.

If I had a nickel for every time I saw text with words like that, I wouldn't have a 2002 Volvo sitting in my driveway.

Why do we use buzzwords and jargon? Some of us might use them to mask our incompetence or insecurity. Some might think those are simply the words of business, especially if their company sells to other businesses rather than to consumers. (But no business truly sells to another business; we all sell to people.)

Those words are the chemical additives of business writing online: You can use them, and maybe one or two used sparingly don't much matter. But use too many of them and they become toxic.

The problem is that business jargon is like New England weather in March: just when you think you are done with the snowstorms, a new one crops up.

91

Yet I'm an optimist. I believe that most of us try to avoid buzzword bloat. We want to be understood. We want in our heart of hearts to sidestep nonwords and clichés and jargon.

Better writing comes from that place of goodness. It means using the right words, choosing real words, and avoiding the temptation of buzzwords.

30

Avoid Frankenwords, Obese Words, and Words Pretending to Be Something They're Not

Avoid Frankenwords—words stitched awkwardly together to create something of a monstrous, ugly, frightening mess. (And, yes, I suppose *Frankenword* is in fact a Frankenword.) For example, you should stay away from words with a shortened form of Armageddon or Apocalypse as a suffix—as in sale-ageddon or snow-pocalypse.

And words like these:

- Amazeballs
- Listicle, charticle, farticle (list-article, chart-article, fake-article)
- Clickability
- Solopreneur
- Awesomesauce
- Fantabulous
- Ginormous
- Chillaxin'

Also avoid words that have additives (many of them have -ize or -ism or -istic fused to the end of them). Like food additives, they make the resulting concoction far less nourishing, and they contribute to a content obesity epidemic: words become fat, bloated versions of themselves.

Finally, run as far as you can from words pretending to be something they are not, particularly nouns masquerading as verbs or gerunds (*workshopping, journaling; leverage; incentivize, bucketize*), and also verbs or gerunds masquerading as nouns (*learnings*).

31

Don't Use Weblish (Words You Wouldn't Whisper to Your Sweetheart in the Dark)

Would you tell your love that you "don't have the bandwidth" for something, or would you say you "don't have the time"?

Would you say, "Let me ping you on that," or would you say, "I'll get back to you"?

Would you say, "You're my top resource," or would you say, "I don't know what I'd do without you"?

Would you put something on his or her "radar screen"? Or "execute on" a promise or commitment?

You get the idea. Weblish words sprouted from technology, and they have no business being applied to people. They sound as if they were being uttered by a robot, not a human being with a brain and soul and actual blood pumping through an actual heart.

32

Know the Difference between Active and Passive Voice

Verbs in a sentence are either active or passive. *Passive* does not mean (as some people believe) the past tense. Rather, *passive* means that something is being done to something, instead of that something doing the action on its own.

Here is an example of the passive voice: Instagram has become popular among pizzerias, and as a result many photos of people eating pizza *are being posted*.

Here is the same sentence written in the active voice: Instagram has become popular among pizzerias, and as a result *people are posting* many photos of themselves eating pizza.

Generally you want to use the active voice, or active writing, instead of the passive voice.

Using the passive voice is not incorrect, but you'll vastly improve your writing just by making your sentences active. Active sounds zippier and more alive. Passive tends to sound a little stilted and awkward, as if you're just learning a new language.

Passive: The video was edited by a guy named Hibachi.

Active: A guy named Hibachi edited the video.

Passive: Duduk theme music is rarely featured on podcasts.

Active: Podcasts rarely feature duduk theme music.

33

Ditch Weakling Verbs

Ditch weakling verbs in favor of bold action words if you want to breathe life into your writing.

Use expressive verbs when you can—when you are describing actions people take or events that occur—because they paint a vivid picture in the reader's mind. With strong verbs your sentences come alive; they throb with a pulse.

> *Instead of:* It might seem like a good idea, but it is probably not in good taste to *put* a QR code on your loved one's tombstone.
>
> *Try:* It might seem like a good idea, but it is probably not in good taste to *etch* a QR code on your loved one's tombstone.
>
> *Instead of:* In his anger, he accidentally *cut* his finger.
>
> *Try:* In his anger, he accidentally *slashed* his finger.

You should strike a balance here, of course, just as you would with most things in life. The trick is to avoid overdoing it with so many action verbs that you give the reader whiplash. That's overwriting, and your text will read like a supermarket romance novel or the diary of a hormonal teenager.

Neither of which, I hope, you'd be intending to emulate.

34

Ditch Adverbs, Except When They Adjust the Meaning

Most writers use adverbs gratuitously, tossing them into text when they really aren't necessary. And so they stand around without much of a role to play, like too many players on a ball field. They add bloat to the field (or your sentence) and pretty soon they get cut from the roster.

I admit that I like adverbs a lot, and I'm probably guilty of using them a bit too much. So I've tried to figure out when adverbs are useful and when they are not. Here's what I've come to: in at least two situations using an adverb makes sense; in at least one, sidestepping them completely makes even more sense. (I'll outline those situations at the end of this rule.)

First, though . . . what's an adverb again? You probably remember from English composition (or if you're like me, from *Schoolhouse Rock* animated shorts on Saturday mornings) that an adverb describes more fully what's going on with the words around it. An adverb often (but not always) ends in *ly*—*gratuitously* and *really* in the first sentence on this page are examples. Or to quote *Schoolhouse Rock*:

Suppose your house needs painting.

How are you going to paint it? That's where the adverb comes in.

We can also give you a special intensifier so you can paint it very neatly or rather sloppily . . .

In his book *On Writing: A Memoir of the Craft*, author Stephen King rails against the unfortunate adverb:

> *The road to hell is paved with adverbs.*
>
> *Adverbs, like the passive voice, seem to have been created with the timid writer in mind . . . With adverbs, the writer usually tells us he or she is afraid he/she isn't expressing himself/herself clearly, that he or she is not getting the point or the picture across.*

Timid writers, in King's view, feel a need to stuff a sentence with explanation rather than relying on a stronger setup (remember *show, don't tell?*):

> *Consider the sentence* He closed the door firmly. *It's by no means a terrible sentence (at least it's got an active verb going for it), but ask yourself if* firmly *really has to be there. You can argue that it expresses a degree of difference between* He closed the door *and* He slammed the door, *and you'll get no argument from me . . . but what about context? What about all the enlightening (not to say emotionally moving) prose which came before* He closed the door firmly? *Shouldn't this tell us how he closed the door? And if the foregoing prose does tell us, isn't* firmly *an extra word? Isn't it redundant?*[1]

So, when do—and don't—adverbs make sense?

Often you can ditch an adverb if you also ditch a weakling verb in favor of livelier one. That makes your sentence briefer and punchier, and it paints a more vibrant picture. For example, instead of saying *production increased quickly*, you might opt for *production surged*.

You should also try cutting an adverb to see whether you absolutely need it to intensify an action or description (because the context doesn't otherwise make the meaning clear). Does dropping the adverb alter the meaning? For example, in my first sentence on this page I needed that adverb *gratuitously* in "Most writers use adverbs gratuitously." Without it the sentence loses its meaning and becomes, "Most writers use adverbs." Well, duh.

Using an adverb to completely change the meaning of an action, and not just augment it, is an approach I like. The juxtaposition and surprise can add a little fizz to a sentence. For example, writing on my own site about how technology has taken some of the anxiety out of growing up, I wrote this: "I can't quite put my finger on it, but somehow that feels . . . justly unfair."

In other words, I don't really think it's unfair; instead, I'm saying there's something kind of awesome about it.

35

Use Clichés Only Once in a Blue Moon

A cliché is an overused simile or metaphor, an unoriginal thought. You already know the clichés of everyday life: a wealthy person who is *rolling in money* and *laughing all the way to the bank.* Probably because he or she *climbed the stairway to success* (or sometimes it's a *ladder* or a *rocky road*).

"Avoid clichés . . . like the plague," advises Toastmasters, a world-wide group that works to improve communication skills. Of course, they say that with tongue firmly planted in cheek (yet another cliché).

The word *cliché* originated in mid-nineteenth-century France, when printers would assemble time-saving blocks of type from the most commonly used word combinations, writes Nigel Fountain in a fun little book on the topic, *Clichés: Avoid Them Like the Plague.*[1] (Those blocks were sometimes called, literally, *stereotypes.*)

"When many of those oldest phrases were first used (in the King James Bible, or by Shakespeare or Milton or Dickens), they were keen insights, new takes, fresh ways of seeing the world. Then someone borrowed them and repeated them. And so did someone else. And pretty soon things just got out of hand," Nigel writes. The hackney horse and carriage were kept for hire, he says, "and thus an overused, unoriginal phrase became hackneyed, tired, overused—a cliché."

Lazy writers use clichés as business platitudes and seem to insert them almost reflexively, without much forethought or intention. Their use is often redundant and vacuous—in other words, they don't add a lot to a discussion. You've probably heard most of them, and they are terrible:

- Open the kimono
- Move the needle
- A *ready, fire, aim* approach
- Take a 30,000-foot view
- Open-door policy
- At the end of the day
- All things being equal
- Drink from the fire hose
- Peel back the onion
- Where the rubber meets the road

In a famous 1946 essay, *Politics and the English Language,* George Orwell took a hard line against clichés: "Never use a metaphor, simile, or other figure of speech which you are used to seeing in print."

But not all clichés are created equal. Sometimes, a well-worn phrase can add some meaning and succinct, colorful, or timeless wisdom. Sometimes it might add charm. And if clichés are used sparingly, they can capture a universal truth nicely. Such phrases or expressions are perhaps better called aphorisms, idioms, or truisms rather than clichés.

So when exactly is that blue moon when it's acceptable to use well-worn phrases?

- When you use them sparingly—more as seasoning than main course.
- When they explain something concisely and act as a kind of universal shorthand: for example, describing a restart as *going back to square one,* or an unexpressed issue as *the elephant in the room,* or the discarding of good ideas along with the bad as *throwing out the baby with the bathwater.*

Here, I've been talking about phrases that are clichés. A related problem is the clichéd concepts used in marketing writing, such as *Content is king,* _____ *is the new black,* and _____ *is dead . . . long live* _____.

But that's a book for another day.

36

Avoid These Mistakes Marketers Make

I've been editing marketing and PR professionals and other business executives for nearly 20 years, mostly at ClickZ and now at MarketingProfs. I just did the math, and at a rate of an article a day that's something like 4,000 pieces of content.

That makes me sound like a bit of a relic. But really what it does is make me pretty familiar with common writing problems that plague marketers and other business professionals. Too often they sacrifice clarity on the altar of sounding professional (with fuzzy thinking, wordiness, conformity, clichés, taking a running start . . . and other things I've talked about in this section and in Part I).

A while ago, I (along with MarketingProfs Director of Publications Vahe Habeshian) started keeping a list of the more common transgressions. Here are the top 17 followed by their anti-wordiness, anti-fuzzy thinking, pro-brevity, pro-clarity equivalents:

1. Ways by which = Ways
2. Continues to be = Remains
3. In order to = To (especially at the beginning of a sentence)
4. There (are) will be times when = Sometimes, At times
5. Despite the fact that = Although, Though
6. At which time = When
7. In spite of = Despite
8. When in comes to = In, When
9. The majority of = Most

10. A number of = Some, Few, Several, Various (or eliminate entirely)

11. When asked = Asked

12. Leverage (as verb) = Use (or Put to Use), Harness, Apply,

13. The same level of = As much

14. While (if not being used to mean during or at the same time as) = Although or Though, Whereas

15. Moving forward = Later, In the future, From now on, Hereafter

16. Centered around = Centered on

17. Try and [verb] = Try to [verb]

Other common errors:

- Use *should have*, not *should of*.
- Keep your verb tense consistent throughout; don't switch around between present, future, past tenses.
- *I versus me.* If you eliminate the other person's name, does the sentence still make sense?

  Not cool: Colin went for a walk with Corey and I.
  Cool: Colin went for a walk with Corey and me.

- *However and independent clauses.* If you use however to join two independent clauses (think sentences) you'll need to use a semicolon—not a comma—before however.

  For example: *I like eating ice cream; however, it doesn't sit well with me.* Better yet, don't try to sound so fancy—use but instead: *I like eating ice cream, but it doesn't sit well with me.*

- *Not only* [x] . . . *but also* [y]. *Not only–but also* are correlative conjunctions (conjunctions that are used in pairs). If the sentence construction isn't parallel when you use these conjunctions—that is, if *x* and *y* are not the same kind of thing (verb, noun, prepositional phrase, etc.)—the reader will be confused for a split second.

  Not cool: Not only will your writing educate readers, but it will also entertain them.
  Cool: Your writing will not only educate [verb] readers [object] but also entertain [verb] them [object].

♦ *[Company, product, other entity] saw a 10 percent improvement in market share, revenue growth of 10 percent, and so on.*

Can a product or company really see anything? Does it have eyes? No, it doesn't. But you do, so you can see how asinine it is to write that an inanimate object saw something.

Instead, try:

[Company, product, other entity]'s market share improved (revenue growth was) 10 percent.

Or try:

[Company, Product, other entity] improved market share (increased revenue) 10 percent.

BTW: Increase 10 percent and increase *by* 10 percent mean the same thing. Use the shorter version unless it sounds really awkward to your ear.

♦ *In terms of.* If you find yourself using *in terms of,* chances are you're not thinking clearly. Rethink what you want to say, and then recast the sentence in a way that eliminates that phrase.

♦ *This/that and these/those.* Unless the antecedent is absolutely clear to the reader, don't use *this, that, these,* or *those*—especially at the beginning of a sentence. If you do use one of them, add a clarification or explanation about, or reference to, the antecedent.

For example: *What credible source supports your main idea? Are there examples, data, real-world stories, relevant anecdotes, timely developments, or new stories you can cite? Those are crucial for building your argument.*

What, exactly, is *those* referring to? Conceivably, it could be any of the nouns in the two questions—or to the questions themselves. So clarify like this: *Those questions* are crucial for building your argument.

♦ *Hyphens after adverbs ending in ly.* If your adverb ends in *ly* and you're building a compound modifier, don't use a hyphen after the adverb. You don't need one. (Unless you're British, in which case you have your own ideas about the English language anyway.) People tend to make this mistake when they try to follow the rule for creating compound modifiers by hyphenating (as in *open-air theater*), but the rule doesn't apply to adverbs that end in *ly*.

Not cool: This is an extremely-simple rule to understand.
Cool: This is an extremely simple rule to understand.

37

Break Some Grammar Rules (At Least These Five)

High school composition classes tend to lump a lot of rules into writing—many of them telling writers what *not* to do. But you're not writing to please your teachers anymore. Many of those prohibitions refer to the so-called mistakes that occur naturally in speech. I encourage you to safely and fearlessly break those rules and to make those mistakes in writing—but only when doing so lends greater clarity and readability.

1. *Never start a sentence with* and, but, *or* because. And why not put *and, but,* or *because* at the beginning of a sentence? Because Ms. Dolan didn't like it? That's the way I heard it, anyway. But now that I'm a grown-up I realize that she was wrong. Why? Because all three can add energy and momentum to a piece. They can keep the action moving from sentence to sentence.
2. *Avoid sentence fragments.* It's perfectly fine to sparingly add sentence fragments for emphasis. At least, sometimes. (Like that.) (And that too.) (And this.)
3. *Never split infinitives.* There's supposedly a rule that says you can't let anything come between *to* and its verb. Mignon Fogarty (who runs GrammarGirl.com) says this is an imaginary rule. She writes, "Instead of 'to boldly go where no one has gone before,' the *Star Trek* writers could just [as] easily have written, 'to go boldly where no one has gone before.'" But they didn't. You,

too, can split if you wish. But be careful not to change the meaning or create too much ambiguity, as Grammar Girl notes:[1]

> *Sometimes when you try to avoid splitting an infinitive you can change the meaning of a sentence. Consider this example:*
>
> *Steve decided to quickly remove Amy's cats.*
>
> *The split infinitive is "to quickly remove," but if you move the adverb* quickly *before the infinitive, you could imply that Steve made the decision quickly:*
>
> *Steve decided quickly to remove Amy's cats.*

4. *Don't end a sentence with a preposition.* It has been said that after an editor changed his sentence so it wouldn't end with a preposition, Winston Churchill quipped, "This is the kind of impertinence up with which I shall not put." Awkward. "This is the kind of impertinence I will not put up with," is perfectly fine.

   One big *unless*: "You shouldn't end a sentence with a preposition when the sentence would mean the same thing if you left off the preposition," Grammar Girl notes. "That means 'Where are you at?' is wrong because 'Where are you?' means the same thing."[2]

5. *Never write a paragraph that's a mere one sentence long.* In school, I was taught to write paragraphs with no fewer than three sentences and no more than seven. Modern marketing has pretty much choked this one dead, because white space helps online readability tremendously.

   But it bears emphasizing: one sentence, set apart, is a great way to make an important point crystal clear.

   I'm not kidding.

38

Learn Words You're Probably Misusing or Confusing with Other Words

S ome words seem interchangeable with others because they sound similar, others because their meanings are confused in everyday usage. Here are some of the most commonly misused words in marketing writing.

First we'll deal with 20 pairs of seemingly interchangeable or similar sounding words. After that we'll take up usage confusion—for example, can you sub *bring* for *take*? Or is it, *may* you sub *bring* for *take*? Or should I simply rephrase the question to avoid revealing my inability to tell the difference?

Similar or Seemingly Interchangeable Words

- **Disinterested:** impartial or unbiased.
- **Uninterested:** don't care.

   You'll notice this confusion in news headlines (kind of like when you are thinking about buying a new Ford Fusion and you suddenly see it all over the place). I saw this headline the other day: "Woman Goes Missing; Disinterested Police 'Guess' She Eloped, Shut Case."[1] That same day, I noticed this: "Eight in Ten SMEs [small and midsize enterprises] Disinterested in Seeking Finance."[2] Both the police and the small business owners were actually uninterested—not disinterested.

- **Accept:** agree to receive, as in "Joakim Noah Reluctant to Accept Praise."[3]
- **Except:** not including (or excluding), as in "Two Charts That Will Enrage Everyone (Well, Except Bankers)."[4]

- **Historic:** having importance in history.
- **Historical:** having taken place in history or otherwise in the past.

    These words seem similar but they are used differently. The former suggests something really important happened, so important that it's worthy of being recorded in history; the latter suggests something that just, well, happened—that it's a factual part of history or the past. David Meerman Scott's book *Marketing the Moon* tells the backstory of an historic undertaking. His unpublished travel diary offers a look at his historical efforts to visit every country in the world.

- **Discreet:** Respecting secrecy or privacy; careful, cautious, diplomatic.
- **Discrete:** Separate and separable; distinct, detached, countable.

    Math geeks might remember that a discrete variable is one that can take on only finite, countable values; it can't express values in between the finite values. You can give your favorite burrito place a 4-star or 5-star rating on Yelp, but you can't give it a 4.9-star rating for that one time they ran out of guacamole (because 4.9 is not in the range of discrete rating choices).

- **Bated:** put in suspension, reduce the intensity of, restrain (think *abated* or *bated breath*).
- **Baited:** to entrap, entice, tease (think *bite*, as in an attempt to get someone to). I always remember this because you could say that the *i* in the middle looks like a worm baited on a hook.

- **Canvas:** Strong cloth (as in TOMS shoes).
- **Canvass:** To examine closely or to ask around (what happens door-to-door every election season).

- **Illicit:** Naughty, illegal, or illegitimate; as in "Silk Road 2.0 Was Hub for Illicit Trade . . ."[5]

♦ **Elicit:** To draw out, extract, or evoke; as in "Ironically, it was also a handy place to elicit Tesco Clubcards."

♦ **Phase:** To schedule in sections (as in *phasing into*), or a specific time period (as in *my foreign phase*). For example: Companies agree to phase out pesticide pet collars.

♦ **Faze:** Throw for a loop, or disturb. As in, "News doesn't faze cats. (Then again, what does?)."

♦ **e.g. (from the Latin *exempli gratia*):** Used to introduce an example. Kids learn this in school as *eggsample*. Which isn't a bad way to remember it. For example: To vastly improve your lead quality use a marketing automation platform: e.g., Marketo, HubSpot, and Act-On.

♦ **i.e. (from the Latin *id est*—and not, like I used to think, shorthand for *in essence*):** Used to clarify or specify. Think about i.e. as if it means *specifically* or *that is*. Use it when you want to clarify or to specify what you were just talking (writing) about. For example: To vastly improve your lead quality, use the favorite marketing automation of small businesses—i.e., HubSpot.

♦ **Flaunt:** To make a showy display.

♦ **Flout:** To disregard a rule or authority. For example: Citizens flout the ban on kite-flying by flaunting colorful kites.

♦ **Insure:** To arrange for compensation in the event of death, injury, or litigation. For example: The company was *insured* against harassment complaints. (In other words, it has to do with insurance.)

♦ **Ensure:** To make certain that something happens. For example: Lead attorney Caroline Price *ensured* that her client received a favorable settlement. (Think of it as *make sure*.)

♦ **Loose:** Unfastened, not fixed in place. For example: "Adult tip" from @HonestToddler on Twitter, "Never pick up a toddler without asking. We're people, not loose change."[6]

♦ **Lose:** Unable to find or detect, to misplace. From "How to Put a Toddler to Bed in 100 Easy Steps," "Adult Tip #93: Tap toddler's back until you lose feeling in your arm and your toddler seems tired."[7]

◆ **Flounder:** To have difficulty doing something
◆ **Founder:** To fail

These are confused as verbs, not nouns; no one confuses the fish called flounder with the founder/entrepreneur (or the founder/blacksmith, for that matter).

◆ **Adverse:** Harmful or negative. For example: FDA warns of adverse effects of new cholesterol drugs . . .
◆ **Averse:** Opposed to, or having an intense dislike of. For example: . . . which makes some heart patients averse to taking them.

◆ **Amoral:** Not concerned with moral standards. For example: Amoral robots pose a danger to humanity.
◆ **Immoral:** Not moral. For example: Hans seems charming and chivalrous, but he is the most immoral character in *Frozen*.

◆ **Nauseous:** Nausea-inducing, poisonous, or gross. For example: a nauseous pile of smelly trash.
◆ **Nauseated:** How that pile of smelly trash makes you feel. For example: sick, wanting to gag, or vomit.

Many people say they are feeling nauseous when they mean they feel nauseated. This is one of those rules that makes me reflect on the fluid notion of language, and whether this one needs to be changed to reflect common usage. I'm probably going to attract a lot of grammar hate for suggesting as much. But there you go.

◆ **Further:** Refers to figurative distance.
◆ **Farther:** Refers to actual, physical distance.

If the kind of distance you're referring to is murky, opt for *further*. For example, Ford's Go Further brand message can be read on two levels: as a literal directive that Ford vehicles are long-lasting and *go farther*, and as a metaphor that Ford itself will exceed expectations.

- **Orient and Orientate:** Both of those verbs mean essentially the same thing, to align or position. I've always hated the clunkier *orientate* and assumed it was wrong. But apparently I'm like a lot of people in the United States who consider *orientate* incorrect, whereas people in the United Kingdom think Americans are wrong in our preference for *orient*. So although I've technically been corrected on this one, I still think *orientate* sounds unnecessarily clunky. Use it at your own risk. At least around me.

- **Horde:** A group of animals or people.
- **Hoard:** A stash of something (or *to* stash something, as a verb).

     Many get this one wrong, and it's commonly confused even by the pros. In a story about a California couple who found more than $10 million in coins on their property in early 2014, a reporter quoted a source speculating on the theory that the coins were possibly stolen from a San Francisco mint. The stolen coins "would have all been mint state, recently struck coins," he said. "But only some of the coins in the Saddle Ridge horde are." *Oops.*

     On the other hand, author Austin Kleon (*Steal Like an Artist*) uses *hoard* correctly when he nicely frames sharing as a social currency: "Almost all of the people I look up to and try to steal from today. .. have built sharing into their routine. . . . They're cranking away in their studios, their laboratories, or their cubicles, but instead of maintaining absolute secrecy and hoarding their work, they're open about what they're working on, and they're consistently posting bits and pieces of their work, their ideas, and what they're learning online."[8]

- **Pour:** to cause to flow.
- **Pore:** a tiny opening; to study something closely.
     (And there's *poor*, too, of course.)

Usage Confusion

- **Fewer versus less.** Use *less* in relation to a single, noncountable item and *fewer* in relation to more than one countable item. So, a good shortcut: if you can count the thing you're referring to, use *fewer*. For example, The couch has less fur on it now that I have fewer dogs.

♦ **They're versus their versus there.** I see *they're*, *their*, and *there* tossed around incorrectly all the time. I think that's simply a matter of not stopping to consider the context in which each is being used. Here's a quick guide:

• *They're* is a contraction for *they are*. Substituting the full phrase before you shorten it will keep you on the right path: *They're* (they are) happy people.
• *Their* shows possession: They're happy people because they have *their* whiskey.
• *There* is a place, either actual or nonspecific. They're happy people because they have their whiskey over *there*. (Easy usage hack: *there* looks like *where*—as in place.)

♦ **Bring versus take.** The verbs *bring* and *take* both involve carrying or conveying something. Usually *bring* refers to something moving toward the speaker or writer (Bring it to me) while *take* suggests movement away from that person (Take it to school). When you order tofu lettuce wraps to go from Ming's, do you order *bring out*? No, you do not, because you are carrying it away. (In the spirit of full disclosure, this is my Achilles heel, as the guy editing this book will tell you.)

A good shortcut: add *go* or *come* to the sentence to figure out whether you should use *take* or *bring*. For example, should you say *bring it to my house* or *take it to my house*? Either can be correct: it depends on whether the person is coming or going to the house. If he's *coming* to the house (coming to you, because you're there), he's *bringing*; if he's *going* to the house (where you aren't), he's *taking*. *Go* pairs with *take*, and *come* pairs with *bring*.

♦ **It's versus its.** *It's* is a contraction of *it is* or *it has*. *Its* denotes possession, but not by a person (in other words, not *his* or *hers*). Maddeningly, Microsoft Word will often autocorrect *it's* to *its*, and vice versa, undermining you even when you have it right to begin with. (It is doing that right now, and my recorrecting Word's autocorrect as I type this is giving my MacBook an aneurism.)

A good shortcut is to substitute *his* (which has no apostrophe) for *its* to see whether not using an apostrophe is correct. For example, The car must have its (his, if the car were male) steering wheel in good working order.

♦ **You're versus your.** Similar to the *it's-its* confusion, *you're* and *your* get confused all the time. *You're* is a contraction of *you are*. Can you substitute *you are* in a sentence and still have it make sense? No? Then use *your*, which shows possession like *their*, *its*, *his*, *hers*, and *ours*.

♦ **Than versus then.** *Than* is used in comparisons; for example, "Money is better than poverty, if only for financial reasons" (Woody Allen) or "A dog is the only thing on earth that loves you more than you love yourself."

   Then relates to time or consequences. For example, "If everyone is thinking alike, *then* somebody isn't thinking" (George S. Patton) or "First learn to scribble, then learn to write."

♦ **Can versus may.** *May* connotes permission (May I drive your antique Nash?*)* while *can* usually denotes ability (Can you drive a stick shift?).

   You might've heard that using *can* to seek permission is wrong and that it should be used only in questioning ability. But it turns out that *can* is perfectly suitable to both situations of ability and permission.

   I wish I could go back and show my ninth-grade English comp teacher that line. She was a real stickler for distinguishing between the two, which made those of us in her classroom sound like British members of Parliament when really we just wanted a bathroom pass.

♦ **Who versus whom.** Use *who* when the word is the subject of a verb: for example, *Who* is the baby-daddy? Use *whom* when the word's the object of a verb: for example, This is my boss, whom I respect. Usually.

   A good grammar hack is to substitute *he* and *him* to see whether you should use *who* or *whom*; *he* would pair with *who*, and *him* (ends in *m*) would pair with *whom* (ends in *m*).

   For example, if you can't decide between *whom do you love* or *who do you love,* substitute he and him and rearrange the words. For example, should it be *him do you love* (or, *do you love him*) or *he do you love* (or, *do you love he*). In this case, you should use whom.

♦ **That versus which versus who.** Use *who* for people, *which* for things, and *that* for either people or things.

I see these abused and confused online all the time, especially when people refer to companies or organizations as *who*, as in *I once worked for a company who manufactured grommets.* Not cool, Internet, not cool.

As for whether you should use that or which in the previous sentence (I once worked for a company that/which manufactured grommets), you'll get heated arguments from the proponents of each. But I'd say don't worry about it; just don't refer to a nonperson as who.

♦ **Whether versus if.** In everyday usage *if* is often used to mean *whether* even though they have different meanings. *If* denotes a condition (if *x* then *y*) and *whether* doesn't; think of *whether* as *whether or not*.

A good shortcut is to see whether you can substitute *whether* for *if*. If, when you do, your intended meaning doesn't change, then use *whether* (because using *if*, in that case, would probably be incorrect). For example, She couldn't decide if/whether wearing black was necessary. Use whether.

Rule 38 was compiled with assistance from Grammar Monster (http://grammar-monster.com) and from Mignon Fogarty's Quick and Dirty Tips (www.quickanddirtytips.com/grammar-girl). Both are excellent resources if you are looking for more grammar advice.

39

Scuse Me While I Kiss This Guy

 Who sang rock the cash-bar? ★

The mutated Clash lyric shown in the preceding graphic is an example of a mondegreen—or a term that results from the mishearing or misinterpretation of a phrase. The graphic is a screen shot of an actual question posed on Yahoo! Answers. (Possibly ironically.)

Well-known examples of mondegreens are *It doesn't make a difference if we're naked or not* (for Bon Jovi's *It doesn't make a difference if we make it or not*), *cross-eyed bear* for *cross I bear*, and perhaps the granddaddy of all mondegreens, *Scuse me while I kiss this guy* (from Jimi Hendrix's 1967 lyric in "Purple Haze," *Scuse me while I kiss the sky*). Which is classic in more ways than one.

Mondegreen was coined by Scottish author Sylvia Write, when her misinterpreting of a Scottish ballad was mentioned in a 1954 article in *Harper's Magazine*. (She misheard *They hae slain the Earl o' Moray and laid him on the green* as *They hae slain the Earl o' Moray and Lady Mondegreen.*)

A subcategory of the mondegreen is the eggcorn, which is also a mishearing or mutation of a phrase, but usually one that makes sense. Examples might be *coming down the pipe* (instead of the actual phrase of *coming down the pike*) and *butt naked* instead of *buck naked*.

Eggcorns—so named by linguist Geoffrey Pullum in 2003 after noting a substitution of *eggcorn* for *acorn*—seem to be growing in number, maybe because many of us writing online are using words and phrases we've heard but have never seen in print, suggests Evan Morris, who writes at the Word Detective website.[1]

Other kinds of wordplay are malapropisms and spoonerisms—which are mostly spoken-word phenomena and (unlike mondegreens or eggcorns) typically (but not always) intentional. A malapropism is when an incorrect word is used in place of a word with a similar sound: Having one husband is called monotony (vs. monogamy). A spoonerism (named for an Oxford prof) is when you switch letters around in a term: Rindercella, Nucking futs, Is it kisstomary to cuss the bride?

So . . . why am I sharing all this with you? For two reasons:

1. To point out that language is a growing, fluid thing. In other words: One day you're an eggcorn. Next day you're . . . well, a tree.

2. Because some of these things really make me laugh when I see them, so I'm sharing the joy.

Many of the following eggcorns are surprisingly common. (The eggcorn comes first, then the correct phrase.)

- You've got another think coming. (You've got another *thing* coming.)
- Nip it in the butt. (Nip it in the *bud*.)
- To the manor born. (To the *manner* born.)
- Abject lesson. (*Object* lesson.)
- Bad wrap. (Bad *rap*.)
- For all intensive purposes. (For all *intents and* purposes.)
- Far be it for me. (Far be it *from* me.)
- Upmost. (*Utmost*.)
- Pot marks. (*Pock* marks.)
- Deep-seeded. (Deep-*seated*.)
- When all is set and done. (When all is *said* and done.)
- Signal out. (*Single* out.)
- Cold slaw. (*Cole* slaw.)
- Duck tape. (*Duct* tape.) (Although apparently this one is controversial in eggcorn circles.)

A curated database of eggcorns is located at eggcorns.lascribe.net. It has more than 600 more of them, if you're so inclined.

40

Limit Moralizing

A void beginning sentences with words that you'd hear from a pulpit, your parent, or a professor. Lose the excessively prescriptive and the moralizing, because it can come off as condescending. Specifically, watch the use of . . .

Don't forget . . .

Never . . .

Avoid . . .

Don't . . .

Remember to . . .

And one so awful I can barely type it:

Always remember to . . .

I admit I've broken this rule a fair amount in this book. Warning someone of the dangers of improper writing without using *never* or *avoid* is hard to do. That's true whether you're warning someone of the possibility of actual death (Never use this curling iron near a bubble bath!) or a metaphorical one (Avoid Frankenwords!).

Prescriptive, how-to instructional writing is one thing; dogmatic copy is another.

The line between preachy and helpful, and educational and flat-out irritating, isn't easy to define. But in your own work be aware that a line does exist. And try—as I have tried here—not to cross it.

Part III

Story Rules

Parts I and II dealt with approaches to writing, as well as some grammar and usage. Part III looks at something more elusive but no less important to modern marketers: the idea of story and storytelling. This is a short section that admittedly only scratches the surface of the topic—a little like chipping away at the visible parts of an iceberg while an even more huge part remains below the surface, unexplored.

But to leave it out of this book entirely felt wrong somehow. So here we are.

First, let's talk about that word *story*.

Story and *storytelling* are two of those words that I sometimes find impossibly squishy in a business context. For me, they often conjure up thoughts more related to performance art than industry.

But here's the thing. Storytelling as it applies to business isn't about spinning a yarn or a fairy tale. Rather, it's about how your business (or its products or services) exist in the real world: who you are and what you do for the benefit of others, and how you add value to people's lives, ease their troubles, help shoulder their burdens, and meet their needs.

At its heart, a compelling brand story is a kind of gift that gives your audience a way to connect with you as one person to another, and to view your business as what it is: a living, breathing entity run by real people offering real value.

In that way, as we wrote in *Content Rules*, your content is not about *storytelling*, it's about telling a true story well.

It's a subtle difference. But the creators of the best content contemplate not just *what* story is worth telling but also *how* to tell it.

41

Tell How You'll Change the World

I'm tempted to insert something here about how stories have a remarkable capacity to stir our souls, to connect us, to shape a kind of shared experience. But because you are human, you know that already, right?

Increasingly, the best marketing has also grokked that, and so in the past few years we've seen an abundance of inspired brand storytelling.

But we've also seen some terrible efforts. Because coming up with your bigger story is (relatively) easy, yet telling a true story in an interesting way "turns out to be about as easy and pleasurable as bathing a cat," says the writer Anne Lamott. (Anne wrote that line in her important book on writing, *Bird by Bird*.)[1]

So how do you pull compelling stories out of your own organization? How do you tell your own brand story in an interesting way that relates to your customer? Start by grokking a few characteristics of a compelling story:

1. *It's true.* Make truth the cornerstone of anything you create. It should feature real people, real situations, genuine emotions, and facts. As much as possible, it should show, not tell. It should explain—in terms people can relate to—how it adds value to the lives of your customers.

2. *It's human.* Even if you are a company that sells to other companies, focus on how your products or services touch the lives of actual *people*. By the way, when you are writing about people, this is a good rule: be specific enough to be believable,

and universal enough to be relevant. (That's a gem from my journalism school days.)

3. *It's original.* Your story should offer a new, fresh perspective. What's interesting about your company? Why is it important? Is it uniquely you? If you covered up your logo on your website or video or blog or any content you've produced, would people still recognize it as coming from you?

4. *It serves the customer.* Your story might be about you, but it should always be told in the context of your customer's life. I've read lots of brand stories that were just flat-out boring (or badly produced) and came off feeling corporate-centric and indulgent because the real protagonist was missing. The best content has your customers in it, so make sure your customer is the hero of your story. Even if you sell something that some might consider inherently boring, like technology—or toasters—focus on how your products or services touch people's lives, or why people should care about them.

5. *It tells a bigger story that's aligned with a long-term business strategy.* We've already talked about aligning story with strategy regarding Cisco's CIO videos. The fast-food company Chipotle is another company that does this really, really well. Its viral video from the fall of 2013, "The Scarecrow," depicts a kind of creepy, dystopian world that makes a heart-wrenching statement about the sorry state of industrial food production.

Alignment of story with strategic goals is critical, so let's look at how it plays out in a few examples, including Chipotle's effort.

In less than a week after its release on Wednesday, September 11, 2013, the Chipotle animated video had attracted 3.1 million views on YouTube, almost 20,000 likes, and more than 4,000 comments. It was picked up by countless media sources (including *Slate*, the *Christian Science Monitor*, and NPR). This past spring (2014), it had over 12.5 million views (and still climbing).[2]

If it's not one of the most poignant moments I've ever seen in marketing, I don't know what is. But Chipotle's effort isn't just a viral video: it is a content marketing play to get people involved in the Chipotle story on a gargantuan scale.

Chipotle might be a fast-food company, but its story isn't about how you can get a cheap but good Mexican lunch on the fly. Instead, it's about what it stands for: good food that's locally and responsibly sourced. That key message (*cultivate a better world*) is incorporated into the video animation.

The *better world* isn't corporate-focused, it's relentlessly customer-focused. It's about a better world for our children, for the chickens and cows, and for us all, in part through linking the content (both literally and figuratively) to the restaurant chain's Cultivate Foundation, which has contributed more than $2 million thus far to help fund initiatives that support sustainable agriculture and family farming.

In other words, Chipotle's animation might be marketing. But it feels more important than marketing.

Similarly, the safety video that plays on Virgin America's in-flight system isn't just a safety video masquerading as a music video. It's also deeply aligned with the brand's musical roots (Virgin sponsors its own music festivals in the United States, the United Kingdom, and Australia, and also sponsors other music-related initiatives). Equally important, it furthers the airline's expressed commitment to "making flying fun again." The message in its safety video might be FAA-required, but the look and feel of it is uniquely Virgin.

Another great big-brand example is from Skype—the video and chat technology company acquired by Microsoft in 2011. Its story, as told in a video called "Born Friends," is about two girls, each born without a full arm. The girls live a world apart but connect via Skype, and eventually meet in person. In other words, Skype's story isn't about call quality or global penetration. It's not about VoIP (voice over Internet protocol) as an alternative to mono-voice telephone communication, and there's not a single mention of data packets. Instead, more subtly, but powerfully, it's about how those things help humans connect with other humans.

Smaller companies may not have the budget of Chipotle, Virgin, or Microsoft, but that's not to say they're necessarily at a disadvantage. The Chicago law firm Levenfeld Pearlstein involved its employees in a unique way to tell its bigger story—and so differentiated itself as a very human and approachable brand. The firm realized (via its Google Analytics reports) that the attorney profile pages were the most visited on its site. (That makes sense, right? If you want to hire an attorney, you want the skinny on exactly whom you are hiring!)

So the firm created a series of partner videos to showcase its lawyers. But here's the interesting part: the firm interviewed its attorneys about unconventional topics, filming their answers to questions like, *what did you want to be when you were little?* And, *if you could time-travel where would you go?* Or, *what is your most prized possession?* That's pretty amazing for a professional services firm, and I love that the videos (and so the firm) make it clear who they are, and who they aren't.

The key takeaway for an organization of any size or stripe: tell that bigger story relentlessly and unwaveringly. Show how you change the world, on a gargantuan scale like Skype (helping human hearts connect with other human hearts) or a smaller scale like Levenfeld Pearlstein (making lawyers real and accessible). As Jay Baer (author of *Youtility*) told me, "Give yourself permission to make your story bigger. Find a way to create content that you love, because no great content was ever created at bayonet point."

Your story should be the steel-infused backbone of whatever content or social media presence you ultimately create. Make sure every person creating content on your behalf is looking through your story lens, metaphorically speaking: Is this telling our bigger story? Is this content steeped in our larger mission?

Incidentally, focusing on your bigger story also helps you communicate strongly what makes you truly unique. (B-school types might call this, depending on the situation, your value proposition, positioning, or unique selling proposition.) And, of course, clearly communicating what makes you unique helps position you for long-term success.

Armed with the fundamentals, ask yourself these questions as a starting point to crafting *your* story:

1. What is unique about our business?
2. What is interesting about how our business was founded? About the founder?
3. What problem is our company trying to solve?
4. What inspired our business?
5. What *aha!* moments has our company had?

6. How has our business evolved?

7. How do we *feel* about our business, our customers, ourselves?

8. What's an unobvious way to tell our story? Can we look to analogy instead of example? (See Rule 19.)

9. What do we consider normal and boring that other folks would think is cool?

10. And most important: relay your vision. How will our company change the world?

That last point is especially salient, because it's the key to your bigger story. *How will you change the world* . . . even a little bit? How will you make it better for all of us?

42

Tell the Story Only You Can Tell

This is actual copy cribbed from the home page of an actual public accounting firm:

> *<Name> is a full-service, certified public accounting practice located in <city> whose objective is to provide timely and accurate professional services. The firm was established in 2002. <Name> is a growing firm and has the capacity available to professionally service new accounts.*

This is an actual press release that landed in my in-box five minutes ago from a Fortune 500 . . . uh . . ."solution":

> *Released today, <name> enables businesses to monitor consumer online chat about their brand and competition, and take action to improve their performance and provide a differentiated customer experience.*

This is from another press release:

> *We have a proven ability to deliver highly impactful results for our clients by leveraging a variety of data sources and advanced analytic approaches.*

This is from a LinkedIn company page profile:

> *<Name> is a contemporary, future-focused consulting services company equipped for the next era of business with the latest in management thinking and enabled by cutting-edge Web technology*

and services. We are building innovative next generation business models and performance improvement capabilities for large corporations highly differentiated by a commingling of new and emerging specialized competencies.

Sometimes it seems as if writers are paid by the buzzword, doesn't it?

The problem with all of these samples is that they could be describing a hundred different companies, rather than one unique company. What sets you apart? What's unique about your story? Don't tell me who you are—*tell me why you matter to me.*

"Start telling the stories that only you can tell, because there'll always be better writers than you and there'll always be smarter writers than you. There will always be people who are much better at doing this or doing that—but you are the only you," author Neil Gaiman said in a 2011 podcast.[1]

43

Voice and Tone

Don't Get Hung Up on Whether Something's Been Said Before—Just Say It Better

In prose, style is a differentiator.

Mark Twain described how a good writer treats sentences:

> *At times he may indulge himself with a long one, but he will make sure there are no folds in it, no vaguenesses, no parenthetical interruptions of its view as a whole; when he has done with it, it won't be a sea-serpent with half of its arches under the water; it will be a torch-light procession.*[1]

He might've just said, as many others have before and since: write with clarity and don't be indulgent. But he didn't. He wrote with a unique perspective and voice.

That doesn't mean you need to be a literary genius, of course. It just means you have to hone your own relatively unique perspective and voice.

Voice (like *story*) is another one of those literary terms that can sound abstract and high-minded in a business context. But the concept is pretty straightforward: your brand voice is simply an expression of your company's personality and point of view. That personality is expressed in how your words sound when they're read, and it's a key differentiator for a company that takes the time to develop it. (And not many do. So you have an opportunity there!)

"Unless you have so-called commodity content—you have to have a unique voice," Andrew Davis, author of *Brandscaping,* told me. "That's part of your hook. That's what makes you different, and how you build relationships with people."

Your unique voice comes from knowing who you are, and who you are not, says Ahava Leibtag, a Web content strategist in Washington, DC, and author of *The Digital Crown.* "Voice grows out of your own brand attributes, and how you want to set yourself apart from your competitors," she told me. Are you sophisticated? Accessible? Fun? Buttoned-up? Serious? Snarky? Reliable? Hipster? Helpful? Pick three or four adjectives that best define you—and write in a way that reflects those attributes.

Voice is also the backbone of the overall look and feel of your content. It informs the overall experience you deliver to people—even in things we don't traditionally think of as marketing.

Here's an example of how Burger King uses voice to convey personality, even in a simple error message (via Ahava Leibtag):

Or consider this mobile update, from the mobile app TalkTo:

In other words, consider your voice as a differentiator across all your customer-focused communications—your website, your mobile updates, and your 404 pages, among other things. But also in your in-store signage, your social presence, and anywhere else you're communicating with people you're trying to reach.

One more thing: consider your tone in various situations as well. Voice doesn't change, but your tone should, depending on the feeling you are trying to convey.

"So your brand can be fun, but if a customer is annoyed, a cheeky email that may come across as cute in one situation may be a major turnoff in another," Ahava said.

Here's an example of how Gogo Inflight maintains the same voice (fun, friendly, accessible) but adjusts its tone to two very different situations. In the first example, Gogo addresses how its mobile in-flight service works—with a fun, friendly voice and decidedly cheeky tone:

| CONNECT | COVERAGE | ABOUT GOGO | CONCOURSE |

How Gogo works

Watch how Wi-Fi takes flight

Congratulations, you're about to witness the birth of the world's first wireless broadband network for inflight connectivity. Watch as a series of simple cell towers are transformed into a revolutionary new form of entertainment — Gogo® – In air. Online.

Technical specifications

Is Gogo fast? Is the sky blue? The Gogo experience is best compared to mobile broadband service on the ground — except with a whole lot more altitude. All you need is a Wi-Fi enabled device, a Gogo account, and a burning desire to access exclusive in-air experiences available only on Gogo.

Related Frequenty Asked Questions

What are the minimum requirements to use Gogo? »

How do I know if my device is Wi-Fi enabled? »

Is it safe to use Wi-Fi in flight? »

How secure is the Gogo Inflight Portal? »

But on Gogo's FAQ page, though it keeps the friendly voice, it drops the cheeky tone in favor of a helpful one (we can help!). Gogo recognizes that people who visit this page are likely annoyed and frustrated by an inability to connect. And cheek, they wisely surmise, would only antagonize.

❚❚ FRANÇAIS

CHAT WITH US ⋮ →   FAQs   E-MAIL US

FREQUENTLY ASKED QUESTIONS ⋮ COMMON TOPICS ⋮ ↓

Ask a question or search our FAQ's below.   →

▾ I bought a Flight Pass on my smart phone. Can I use it on my laptop or tablet?

Flight Passes which have been purchased while on your smart phone cannot be used for laptop or tablet access. If you want to be able to switch between 2 or more types of devices, you will need to purchase your pass from the tablet, laptop, or the ground. If you're in flight and would like to upgrade your pass, <u>chat</u> with us - we can help!

44

Look to Analogy instead of Example

As you think of ways to tell your story, consider that the way you tell it doesn't have to be original to the whole world. As professor Mason Cooley has said, "Art begins in imitation and ends in innovation."[1] So look at what other people or organizations are doing—sometimes, even those outside of business entirely.

Marketing expert Seth Godin makes the same point repeatedly, and it's one I also espouse. Don't wait for a case study in your specific industry or field to prove the effectiveness of a marketing tactic. Rather, heed what Godin says on his blog: "Innovation is often the act of taking something that worked over there and using it over here."[2]

Consider some of the content examples in this book: Virgin dances to MTV's tune for its in-flight safety briefing; HubSpot borrows a page from *People* magazine (see Rule 74). And Massachusetts congressional candidate Carl Sciortino fashions a new mode of political campaigning when he patterns his video after storytelling.

In a bid for the Massachusetts Fifth District congressional seat, Sciortino was one of seven Democrats running in a special election in December 2014, the result of a sequence of events that were set off when John Kerry became U.S. secretary of state.

Sciortino is openly gay (he married his partner 10 days before the election), and the story in his ad plays with the idea of Carl coming out to his conservative Tea Party father. Not as a gay man, but as a Massachusetts liberal.

In other words: Gay? NBD. Liberal? Ouch.

"He's been this way for 35 years," Pops grouses in the video, in a kind of mock, kids-say-the-darndest-things despair.

Sciortino was a dark-horse candidate and ultimately lost. Still, the effort received national attention (the *New York Times*, the *Daily Beast, Hardball*). The *Washington Post*'s Aaron Blake called it "one of the more interesting campaign ads we've seen in a while." MSNBC's *All In* host Chris Hayes tweeted about it to his 250,000 followers.[3]

At the time, political pundits praised it for the way the ad sets up Sciortino as principled but loveable, in the vein of former Massachusetts senator Ted Kennedy: People might disagree with him, but they still seem to respect him.

At the heart of the video is a compelling narrative (and not just a political slogan). A son and father disagree; somehow, they make it work.

Think about this: Sciortino could've created a typical ad outlining what makes him different. He could've listed his progressive values, outlined his belief in the right to choose, and so on. Would that have been compelling? Nope. As my friend and video genius Tim Washer says: "That isn't really a story." Because it wouldn't get people emotionally invested. It wouldn't make Sciortino relatable. It would've lacked heart.

The bigger story, of course, is Sciortino's character. The video gives you a richer, fuller sense of who he is as a candidate. And it also subtly suggests that Sciortino is a person who can work within a structure where people don't agree with him—perhaps even if they aren't related to him.

Again: What's new in your market . . . is new. Instead of relying on the typical formulas of political campaigns, Sciortino borrows a page from storytellers. He scripts his own narrative.

Most organizations, brands, bands, churches, nonprofits, politicians, and the like aren't always there: they still see content creation as a box to check on some broader marketing campaign. But Sciortino doesn't squander his opportunity. He takes a compelling story and plops it right in the lap of politics.

And one more thing, as it applies to Sciortino (and more generally, too): innovation is more about brains than budget. Sciortino's video didn't have a big budget behind it, yet it's effective because it tells a true story well.

Q: How many campaign managers are out talking to storytellers today to replicate some of this magic?

A: All of them.

Part IV

Publishing Rules

Many companies have adopted the we're-all-publishers-now mantra—but without a clear understanding of the ground rules of publishing.

No matter what kind of content marketers are charged with creating, they can learn much from the publishing world—in particular from journalism. Thinking like a publisher is simply not enough; you also need to *act* like one.

Not long ago I noticed that a company had co-opted some content that we at MarketingProfs had created; the word thieves had scrubbed it free of our branding and other identifiers, and then passed it off as their own.

That sort of thing happens all the time on the Web, I know: bots constantly scrape content and republish it elsewhere with no regard for copyright or author.

But this situation felt a little different to me, because the piece that was lifted was something our team was particularly proud of: we had invested long hours in creating what we thought was nothing short of brilliant (and, incidentally, it also drove business effectively for us). In other words, the theft felt more like an ethical violation than straightforward copyright infringement. And it felt more personal because it was the theft of an idea and execution that we had spent long hours honing—rather than just a cut-and-paste of a blog post, say.

Content creation and social media are an opportunity for brands . . . a huge one, in fact. But, when it's done incorrectly (as it was by those co-opters), it's a potentially huge fail that could tick people off—and also damage your reputation, your brand, and your business.

Contently, a content management platform, suggests that those creating content on behalf of brands should actually adhere *more strictly* to standards than mainstream journalists do, because people are naturally skeptical of something produced by a brand.

"Content marketing should seek to adhere to stricter standards of reporting than traditional journalism, due to its different legal position and increased commercial motivations," Contently cofounder Shane Snow writes in a kind of code of ethics manifesto.[1] He implores content creators and brand publishers alike to adhere "to journalism's core values of honesty, integrity, accountability, and responsibility."

I'd also add *generosity* to Shane's list. *Generosity* might not be an original tenet of journalism, but it's a necessary mind-set for modern-day content creators: you need to freely and generously provide content that has real value for your audience. That kind of makes it easy for people to trust you and believe you—and also rely on you. You want your content to be so useful that they *thank you* for generously producing and providing it.

Part IV of *Everybody Writes* offers guidelines on how to act like a publisher by adapting some best practices from journalism, including a broader awareness of the responsibility and privilege that come with building an audience. It starts by looking at the nature of journalism within an organization (*brand journalism*), and then offers some guidelines for anyone who creates content on behalf of a brand, whether that person is J-school-trained or not.

45

Wait. What's Brand Journalism?

Some companies are looking toward traditional journalism to fill the gaping content maw; they are hiring those trained in J-school tactics, such as reporting and storytelling, as in-house *brand journalists*.

A brand journalist or corporate reporter works inside the company, writing and producing videos, blog posts, photos, webinars, charts, graphs, e-books, podcasts, and other information that delivers value to your market.

Such content creators convey your company's true story in a compelling way by uncovering the stories about your brand and the way your customers are using your products and services. They narrate those stories in a human, accessible way, and they spark conversation about your company, customers, and employees.

In short, brand journalists bring a reporter's sensibility to your content—an editorial approach to building a brand. That's especially useful when we all need to place the needs of our audience first and rise above our corporate-centric messaging. Journalists' innate understanding of audience means that every time they sit down at their desks to create content, a little voice in the back of their head reminds them: *Nobody has to read this.* That kind of pressure on your content-creation efforts can only benefit your brand and enhance your integrity.

But Is It Really Journalism?

This might be a good time to ask, but what about that integrity issue? Is a brand journalist really a journalist?

In my mind, brand journalism *is* a kind of journalism, even if it isn't impartial. For example, a brand journalist wouldn't produce something negative about the company; a traditional journalist would. So I'm not suggesting that brand journalists produce traditional news reporting. They are different, albeit similar, things. And we need both in our world.

I like *brand journalist* mostly as shorthand: it's easy for companies and others to grok the meaning at a glance. It immediately suggests what the role is . . . as well as what it isn't.

An embedded corporate journalist is often more of a storyteller than a straight news reporter. All journalists (whether brand-side or not) deal in facts—they tell true stories well. "Facts are the pillars of any good reporting," Jesse Noyes, a former reporter for the *Boston Business Journal,* told me. He worked as a corporate reporter at Eloqua (now Oracle Eloqua) and now heads up content marketing at marketing technology company Kapost.

But what Jesse says is especially true for company reporting. "What you're after is a story that connects the fact-finding process in a visceral, meaningful way. That means digging up the facts, but also shining a light on the decision-making, the personalities involved, the raw human emotion that goes into any fact-based story," Jesse said.

The term *brand journalism* was coined in 2004 by Larry Light, then McDonald's chief marketing officer, who said in a speech at an industry event that McDonald's had adopted it as a new marketing technique. The term has evolved since then, as have the approaches and goals for the media that's created inside a company. But the basic idea of customer-driven versus corporate-driven marketing remains fundamental.

The notion of taking a journalistic approach to content creation has gained steam over the past few years. HubSpot hired journalist Dan Lyons (*ReadWrite, Newsweek, Forbes*) as its so-called marketing fellow. Qualcomm hired former *USA Today* editor Michelle Kessler to head up Qualcomm's content strategy. Others—such as Boeing, Home Depot, General Electric, and the Florida Travel and Tourism Board—have hired journalists to either head up or contribute to the content charge.

"Brands are hungry for content, and journalists are good at creating content," Dan Lyons told me. "They are natural storytellers who know how to spot a story and how to tell it effectively. They also bring an outside perspective and a touch of skepticism, which may or may not be helpful, depending on the company."

How Brand Journalism Works

A good example of what the results might look like comes from GE, which publishes *GE Reports* (www.gereports.com), a daily online magazine that features stories and opinions about innovation and science and technology. It looks not unlike, say, *Popular Science.* I just went to the GE Reports site and found myself engrossed for a few minutes in a story about something called ZeeWeed Membrane Bio-reactor, a GE-developed filtering membrane that is saving a New Zealand volcanic lake from gross algae explosions. Who knew?

In an e-book he created for HubSpot,[1] Dan Lyons points out that GE's approach is one of four that are common in brand journalism today:

1. *Generating brand awareness.* The effort is largely centered on creating awareness of the company's larger story, because you want people to know about and be familiar with your company—what it is and what it stands for. You're not trying to generate sales directly from such articles.

   Example: The focus of *GE Reports* is on innovation at GE. It goes well beyond any effort to sell you lightbulbs, jet engines, or financial services.

2. *Producing industry news.* You write reports and articles about your own company and its industry, creating coverage that supplements the work of mainstream media (and sometimes attracts its attention so that mainstream reporters cover your story as well).

   Example: Intel Free Press is a technology news site Intel launched in 2010. Free Press is "a way to cover stories that aren't being covered elsewhere, and possibly to persuade mainstream outlets to pick up those stories themselves," Dan Lyons writes.

3. *Creating and sponsoring.* When you want to establish your company as a thought leader, you can create a vendor-agnostic, independent site to help people you are trying to reach.

   Example: Adobe's CMO.com. Also, American Express's OPEN Forum, which publishes information designed to help small business owners. And OpenView Venture Partners, which publishes the OpenView Labs site, the tag line of which is "helping companies grow."

   Notice how that tag line says *companies* and not *our portfolio companies?* That's because the OpenView Labs appeals to all growing businesses—not just the companies OpenView funds. In other words, it takes a journalistic, neutral approach to its marketing via the site—and in doing so taps into its bigger story, as we talked about in Part III.

4. *Generating leads.* You can use content as a way to generate leads, which might then be converted into customers. HubSpot is a prime example here; its content is created with lead generation in mind. Most articles or posts on its blog include a call to action for an offer that is behind a registration gate (the visitor must provide an email address to receive the offer). Those registrations generate leads, which are passed on to the sales organization.

Of course, there are hybrids of the four models: often, lead generation efforts and subscription models are paired with each approach. But that's a pretty comprehensive (if simplified) look at how brand journalism might work.

Hiring journalists to work on behalf of your company has pros and cons, Dan Lyons told me. On the plus side, journalists have been trained to work fast, and they can produce lots of content in a short period of time. And because of the contraction of the news industry, lots of well-trained reporters are seeking alternatives to traditional jobs.

On the down side, though, some journalists are accustomed to having lots of independence. They might not like collaborating. And because they tend to be skeptical, even cynical, there might be some issues with fitting into company culture. "Both parties need to be aware of potential pitfalls, and both sides need to be able compromise a bit," Dan said.

46

Tell the Truth

Creating content on behalf of brands requires you to be scrupulously trustworthy. You need to be honest with your readers.

That means you tell the full truth, with fairness, integrity, and accountability—just as traditional journalists are expected to do. It also means that you credit sources; ground your content in data; acknowledge any bias that may compromise your point of view; link to sources generously; cite reliably; disclose all connections, sponsors, conflicts, or potential biases; and limit the number of anonymous sources. (See specific sections in the book for more on all those.)

At the same time, telling the truth means featuring real people, real situations, genuine emotions, and actual facts. Give examples and get interviews and perspectives outside of your own—and your company's.

As much as possible, your content should show, not tell. It should show your product as it exists in the world—in the form of customer stories, outside perspectives, examples and narratives, and good old-fashioned reporting.

"I still believe the old thing about reporters doing best work when they get away from their desks and out into the world," Dan Lyons told me. "Also I think including other voices into your content is a way to raise awareness of your brand."

Such an approach isn't just a great way to tell a truer story. It's also a great way to keep your content focused on the customer, and less on the company.

47

See Content Moments Everywhere

When the world's third-largest software company, Oracle, acquired content management company Compendium in October 2013, I first heard about it when Jesse Noyes emailed me an hour after the news broke, asking me for commentary on the acquisition for a piece he was putting together.

Jesse, a former journalist, heads up content at Kapost, a competitor to Compendium. That morning, he also took the opportunity to let me know that his boss, Kapost CEO Toby Murdock, had already formulated and published his early thoughts on the acquisition on the Kapost blog.

See what happened there?

Kapost was the one that broke the story to me and to others less than an hour after it happened. Understanding that this news was a big deal in the content marketing world, Kapost moved swiftly and was able to . . .

- Use news of a competitor to insert itself into the heart of a story that essentially had nothing to do with it.
- Use the news to be a thought leader, by expanding the immediate news story into a larger trends piece that has broader appeal.
- Capture early social love from influencers, and connect with influencers as well as industry analysts to offer them a platform for further commentary.
- Potentially earn attention from mainstream media looking for perspectives on the news within the industry.

Having a nose for a story, and making it more broadly relevant to audiences, is something journalists are trained to do. But there's a great lesson in there for businesses, too: content moments are everywhere; you just have to know to look for them. Sometimes, that means being part of breaking news. But it also means tapping into broader trends (more on that in a minute).

Kapost's effort is a great example of what marketer and author David Meerman Scott calls *newsjacking*—injecting yourself into a breaking news story. Kapost's move is not unlike an event David talks about in his book of the same title (*Newsjacking*, John Wiley & Sons, 2011). He writes that Joe Payne, former CEO of marketing software provider Eloqua, newsjacked the 2010 story about Eloqua competitor Market2-Lead's being purchased by (again!) Oracle. Joe sprung into action and quickly composed a blog post on the news, as Toby did three years later for Kapost.

Much as the leaders of many companies want to use their content marketing programs to become thought leaders, a key piece of being a thought leader is to . . . well, *lead*!

That means looking at the news cycle for opportunities to become part of developing trends and events. Timing is key here, because it's important to catch a news story just as it's developing, not as it's dying. David Meerman Scott offers a visual on the key time to newsjack:

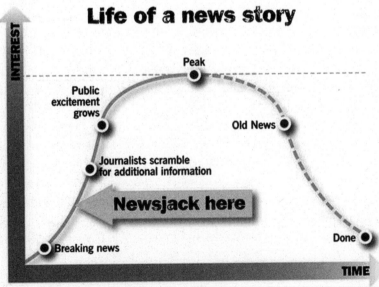

Source: Reproduced by permission of David Meerman Scott.

I engaged in newsjacking firsthand not long ago, when Facebook's chief operating officer, Sheryl Sandberg, launched her Ban Bossy campaign in March 2014. I wrote up my early thoughts within hours of hearing of the joint effort by Sheryl and the Girl Scouts of America to ban the word *bossy* via a sweeping social media campaign, media blitz, and content program.

The resulting post not only ignited unprecedented traffic and engagement on my own site but also attracted mainstream media attention from National Public Radio's San Francisco affiliate and the Associated Press. Ultimately my teenage daughter was interviewed for a story that ran on ABCNews.com.

Because content moments are everywhere—and can happen at any time—you have to be ready to pounce at a moment's notice. Kapost's Jess Noyes puts it this way: "You have to get things done on a tight deadline."

That means sussing out the story and the players involved, and actually writing it up all within a day, Jesse said, adding, "Back in my newspaper days I would sometimes turn in two or three stories a day. That's a highly transferable skill in the marketing world."

Newsjacking is one approach. But the *see content moments everywhere* mantra also applies to trends or events outside of your specific industry.

One great example is the New York Public Library's literature-inspired March Madness smackdown on Instagram, which pitted famous authors against one another in a series of tournament brackets. Followers could vote on their favorites (Judy Blume versus Beverly Cleary, Gore Vidal versus Norman Mailer, and so on), and the winners advanced toward the finals.

PropertyCasualty360.com, an insurance industry trade publication, created a piece called "4 Ways Insurance Might Respond If Godzilla Attacks,"[1] a lighthearted but nonetheless serious look at property and casualty issues caused by catastrophes. The site published the piece to coincide with the release of the latest Godzilla remake in the spring of 2014 and includes this setup: "Ever think about policy wording, exclusions, and ISO forms when watching a summer blockbuster? You're not alone."

What does Dr. Seuss or David Sedaris have to do with basketball? What does Godzilla have to do with insurance? Nothing, really. But they are timely and fun twists on popular culture—content moments that the NY Public Library and PropertyCasualty360 identified and seized.

48

Post News That's Really News

Companies often spin internal developments as news that's worth reporting on, even though the developments are not really all that interesting. For example, they'll write a blog post announcing a minor product upgrade, or a new hire, or something so boring I can't even think of it to use as an example right here . . . because I delete it without reading it when it arrives in my in-box.

I'm not sure exactly why companies do this. Is it because they are trying to placate a corporate executive with a giant ego coupled with minuscule content sensibility?

Or because they compensate poor PR people based on a sliding scale of how much they annoy people?

I don't know. But I do know this: don't be that guy.

In his seminal book on journalism, *Writing to Deadline*, Donald Murray offers a pointer on how to find the focal point (or lead) in a story: "What would make the reader turn and say to her husband, 'Now listen to this, Ira . . . '?"[1]

Murray isn't talking about how to discern what's worth sharing and what isn't, but it's a good filter to use. You might not be targeting Ira's wife as your reader, but consider her a proxy for your own reader by asking, *would the reader find this useful to know?*

If the answer is yes . . . it's news worth sharing. If the answer is no . . . well, issue a press release if you must. But your mission as a marketer is to make sure it stays off your company blog and archived in the Press or Media section of your website as background for journalists, researchers, analysts, or other interested parties.

49

Biased *and* Balanced

Seek Out Opposing Viewpoints

"There's a name for something with a single point of view: it's called a press release," Joe Chernov, VP of content at HubSpot, once told me.

What does that mean for you? It means you should incorporate multiple perspectives when the issue lends itself to doing so. At the very least, don't ignore the fact that other points of view might exist; to do so makes your reader not trust you.

As I said right up front in this section on publishing rules, trust is critical in publishing, and you want your readers to know that you're watching out for them. To quote Hemingway: "The most essential gift for a good writer is a built-in, shockproof, shit detector." And you need to protect your readers from content that stinks.

Does that mean you should mention your competitors? Maybe. At the very least, acknowledge that they exist, or that alternative viewpoints might exist.

I like the approach of being biased *and* balanced, which sounds paradoxical but isn't. In fact, it's a hallmark of good brand journalism.

Biased and balanced coexist even in traditional journalism.

"The *New Republic* was always a biased magazine," Dan Lyons said in an email interview. And so was *Forbes*, where Dan worked as senior editor.

"At *Forbes* we were not allowed to write stories that said, 'On the one hand this, on the other hand that. . . ,'" he said. "We were under orders to have an opinion, to take a side and defend it. But we were also expected to 'fight fair,' meaning you should be honest, and acknowl-edge all the facts, and then say why you believe what you do."

One hypothetical example might be this, Dan said: "Apple stock is a bargain right now, and you should buy it. Why? Apple is about to release a bunch of great new products in the second half of this year and when it does the stock will soar. To be sure, the counterargument is that Apple's growth has slowed, and some critics think it will never be a growth stock again. However, I think the new iWatch could sell XX number of units at XX dollars, and this would be a huge shot in the arm to Apple's revenues."

Opposing views are one thing, but the competitor issue is difficult for a lot of companies. Ultimately, it's a call each has to make on its own.

"Personally, I think it would be a great thing to call out a competitor that has done something really amazing and good, and to praise them," Dan said. "I think this would reflect well on your brand and would earn the admiration of potential customers.

"Let's have our corporate blogs be places where we exchange ideas and learn from each other, out in public," Dan said. "Let's debate issues, share best practices, and remember that we're all trying to find the best way to serve customers, so if we can learn from another brand, or they can learn from us, that's great. That's sort of the ultimate vision for what a corporate blog could accomplish.

"But in reality," he added, "I imagine very few brands would do this."

The flip side of this approach—in other words, calling out a competitor for a misstep and criticizing them—is most definitely a bad idea. Don't do it. You risk looking small and petty, with a mean little heart of stone.

50

Nonobvious Interview Tips

In my first job, I was a new reporter covering the banking and real estate industries for a weekly newspaper in Boston. Because I was so young and the topics I was writing about felt foreign to this humanities major, I tried to fake a level of comfort so I wouldn't seem dumb.

When, for example, I'd ask a banking executive my carefully constructed question about the lingering aftereffects of the housing boom in New England, and he'd answer, his response would sound utterly alien to my ears—he might as well have been telling me how to resolve a vector into Cartesian coordinates. Though I'd have no idea what he was talking about, I would be too embarrassed to ask for clarification. Because of that fear-of-looking-dumb thing.

Since then, I've learned that it's far better to embrace your ignorance and admit what you don't know. (I suppose that is true in interviewing *and* in life, now that I think of it.) Because if you don't understand it well, you can't explain it to your audience.

Content marketers who have been tasked with interviewing someone with deep expertise in a subject might have a sense of what I'm talking about here. It's a little daunting to admit, "Wait, you lost me there," but you are far better off being up front about it. And (as I ultimately realized), subject-matter experts generally love to explain what they know.

Before offering interviewing tips, I'm going to assume that you've got the basics already covered—for example, you've at least googled the person, you have the gist of the issue at hand, and you've researched what he or she has previously said or written on the topic.

In other words, you've prepared. Here are seven less obvious techniques to help hone your interviewing skills.

1. *Be an advocate for your audience.* What are you trying to get out of the interview for the benefit of your audience—the people who will consume this piece of content you're creating as a result of an interview? If it's something specific, make sure you open with a question that answers the biggest question you want answered on behalf of your listener or reader.

    Your number one goal is to be useful to your readers or listeners—so make sure you are an advocate for them, and get what they need.

2. *Don't worry about being an ignoramus.* I said as much earlier: ask for clarification about what you don't know. If you're dealing with a highly technical or intricate issue, it helps to ask, how would you explain it to your mom or dad? That's not to say mom and dad are stupid, but they are a handy stand-in for an audience that would benefit from a plainer explanation. Another good question to ask is something like this: could you give me an example of how this might play out with a customer?

3. *Go for one-on-one conversation.* Phone, video, or in-person interviews feel more natural and loose when it's just you and the expert—with no PR reps or assistants or note-takers listening in. Having a silent participant is just weird, even if that person has a job to do there. His or her presence hinders the back-and-forth flow of conversation and often makes the expert feel self-conscious, resulting in an unnecessarily constrained and forced exchange.

    The same goes for group interviews. The conversation can easily degenerate into one-upmanship, for example, or it can turn more formal and restrained than a one-to-one chat would be. Moreover, including colleagues or partners in the interview can also be confusing for the interviewer (who said what again?).

4. *Get the spiel out of the way first.* Experts who have had corporate PR training sometimes rely too much on Frankenspeak or canned, prepared responses. In those situations, I find it's best to just let them get it out of their systems—and then ask

follow-up questions to elicit less practiced, less wooden responses.

5. *Converse, don't interview.* The best podcast hosts converse with their guests instead of interviewing them. They start out with a planned question or two and then let the response dictate the conversation. "Be prepared, but don't read off a script," suggests Kerry O'Shea Gorgone, who hosts the weekly MarketingProfs podcast, *Marketing Smarts.* "Conversations aren't scripted, and you want an interview to feel like a conversation."

   If you're trying to get specific information out of an interviewee—for example, for a bylined article or a blog post— you'll want to guide the conversation a bit, of course. Don't just let it wander off into a tangential rabbit hole.

   To keep things on track but still free-flowing, practice what my friend (and former MarketingProfs podcast host) Matthew T. Grant calls *laser listening*: listening for threads of the response to naturally pick up in a subsequent question. Don't just jump to the next question on your list just because, well, it's on the list.

6. *Superlatives can make for great interview fodder.* Questions like, "What's the more interesting/best/baddest/most controversial/greatest/worst" can give you some great material to work with. Other favorite questions of mine: How did you get interested in this line of work/program/etc. . . . or How did you wind up here?

   People's journeys are always interesting—both to themselves and to others. And they can reveal some interesting bits of color about a person.

7. *Shut up already.* Your job is to draw the interviewee out, so try to speak less and let the other person speak more. Try not to interrupt unless it's to ask a clarifying question. "An interview show isn't about the host, it's about the guests," says Kerry O'Shea Gorgone. "Interjecting without having something truly worthwhile to add can disrupt the flow and cause the guest to lose her train of thought."

   That said, you might have the kind of interviewee who in turn is not shutting up or doesn't seem to be making much headway toward giving you what you need. In that case, you'll have to steward his or her end of the conversation more aggressively. You are there as an advocate for the reader or listener, and so you need to stay in charge.

If you want to record interviews, plenty of tools are available. (Skype is free and easy to configure; Camtasia is another option. For more content creation tools, see Part VI). But I am a fan of simple note-taking—in my case, with a Sharpie in a notebook. For some reason, recording someone's words with my own hand also captures a bit of the mood, and it allows me to quickly jot asides in the margins that I can refer to later—as follow-up questions, or as ideas I might want to include in a final written post or article.

Maybe that's hopelessly old-school, but I like the visceral feeling of it.

51

Fact-Check

Fact-checking sounds about as much fun as matching a laundry basket full of socks. But, really, it's at the root of your credibility. You want your readers to trust your content, and (importantly) to share it with all the confidence that what you say is true.

I'm imagining your retort: *But we aren't a news site.*

It's not just news sites that need to get the facts straight. Mistakes undermine your brand's credibility in the eyes of any reader, no matter the subject.

When I say *fact-check,* by the way, I'm talking about obvious things—like the spelling of proper names or company names or titles and the rest (like making sure links point to where you expect them to). It pains me to have to say this, but my name gets botched all the time in social media, and I see others suffering a similar fate. (I've seen references to *Slideshare, Slide Share,* and *Slide share* all within the same article. I've had our company called *MarketingProfs, Marketingprofs,* and *Marketing Profs* all within the same article, too. And one time, a writer called us *Marketing Land.* Which was just puzzling.

So double-check proper names and company names and use them consistently and correctly. Not to do so is just sloppy.

At the same time, think beyond the obvious spelling errors, and make sure all of the facts in your content can be backed up by reliable sources. Question every statistic, number, or bold fact, and make sure you can back it up.

You need to fact-check even if you are just curating information published by others; let it become a source of pride for you, just as it is for Upworthy.com. Here's what Matt Savener, Upworthy's copy chief, wrote in a February 2014 post, "Why We Fact-Check Every Post on Upworthy":[1]

> *We take the trust our community places in us very seriously. Credibility is perhaps the most important trait of great curation. So don't worry about spreading bad info. If it says "Upworthy," you can share it with confidence, knowing that it checks out.*

I like how Upworthy considers credibility a cornerstone of its publishing. It's a great model for any of us to follow.

52

Approach Content with 'Mind Like Water'

A lifetime ago, when I was covering town-planning board meetings for a local newspaper, I arrived in the newsroom very late one night and told the night editor that there wasn't a single thing to report on, because no decisions had been reached by the board. The editor—who I'm certain ate cigarettes for breakfast—schooled me thus: there's always a story there, he said, even if it's not the one you were expecting to write.

So your boring technology product? Your services firm? Your regulated industry that precludes you from talking about certain specifics? The mind-like-water content creator finds the crevices that the stories flow into and reside in.

(Also, whatever you sell or market can't possibly be as dull as town-planning board meetings, and I found plenty to say after that night.)

I said it here already: content moments are everywhere. Companies so often fear that they don't have anything interesting to share. In truth, though, every one of us has a great font of inspiration right in front of us, if we only train ourselves to see it. As the designer Michael Wolff says, "What already exists is an inspiration."

Consider the content-creation prompts that follow, and for more content development tools, see Part VI:

- What's commonplace to you that might be interesting to others?
- What events outside our industry or in the larger world might serve as inspiration?

- Get out of the office: trade shows, clients, and partners all offer content opportunities.
- Draw offbeat analogies from your own life or interests.

A post that copywriter Tom Bentley wrote for MarketingProfs is an example of that last item: "Mark Twain's 10-Sentence Course on Branding and Marketing."[1] Or the way Jason Miller, a content marketing strategist at LinkedIn, frequently draws from his love for metal music, as in "5 Rock n Roll Quotes to Inspire Content Marketing Greatness."[2]

53

Seek Out the Best Sources

Newspaper reporters go to the scene of an incident to report what happened; in the business world, you should, too. Metaphorically speaking.

Are you blogging about a new technology? Talk to the guy who developed it, not the PR or marketing person promoting it. My newspaper editors used to tell me this: find the person standing closest to the center of a story.

Be aware of the difference between *on the record, for background,* and *off the record*:

- On the record means you can quote sources freely and use their full names for attribution.
- For background (also called unattributable) means you can use the material but not attribute it to a specific person or source.
- Off the record means you can't write about the details or quote the person sharing them. The information you're given is meant to be confidential.

54

Be Aware of Hidden Agendas

If you interview someone for a story, be clear about the agenda that is potentially fueling that person's point of view.

Often in business that means you should follow the money. Who butters his bread? Is she a competitor? Investor? PR professional retained to maintain a specific point of view?

The person might still be credible as a source—in fact PR folks can be awesome background sources—but you need to be aware of agendas.

And if you decide to use the material, disclose the source and potential vested interests or conflicts of interest.

55

Cite as You Write

Proper citation is rooted in respect for other people's work and it allows your readers to refer to the original source of your information if they so wish. Think of it as a giant *thank you* to the people who said something before you did, or helped advance your thinking on an issue.

Seek out primary, not secondary sources. A primary source is an original research project, or the originator of an idea or statement. A secondary source quotes the original source.

Citing the original source is maybe a big *duh*. But I'm always surprised by how often companies link to a secondary source (merely another site or writer who's sharing an article) instead of the original. The credibility you gain is worth the extra click or two to track down the primary source.

Quoting or linking to primary sources isn't just good ethics, it's likely your information will be more accurate, too, since it hasn't been inadvertently reinterpreted. Generally, the more recent the research, the more appealing it is. Try to avoid anything older than four years, since it's likely to be stale. In some fast-evolving industries—mobile or social media, say—avoid anything more than two years old.

Wikipedia is not a credible source—even according to Wikipedia itself.[1] But it's great for anecdotal or background information, and it can be a handy place to find links to other sources, including original ones.

How does citation apply to content creators?

As an example, if you use an infographic, cite the original source and link to it, even if you first discovered it elsewhere. If you create that infographic based on someone else's data, say that too. Also, if you interview someone and use what she says either directly or indirectly, attribute the ideas to that person, even if you don't use her exact words.

You should formally cite a work if you're creating a heftier content asset—say, a book like this one, an e-book, an annual report, a research paper, or a white paper. In those cases you have various citation styles to choose from (including those recommended by the *Associated Press Stylebook*, the *Chicago Manual of Style*, and so on). Which one you use isn't all that important; what matters is that you pick one and use it consistently. (Tools like Son of Citation Machine [citationmachine.net] can spit out a properly formatted citation after you plug in some basic information about what you're referencing and where you found it.)

For more casual pieces—for example, a blog post or similar item—you can simply provide the name of the original source (the publication, website, magazine, and so on) as an aside. Include the author's name if there is one. If the source is an online source, include a specific link as well—that of the specific blog post, not just the blog home page.

For slide presentations, cite the author right alongside the content you used any time you use someone else's ideas, text, or images on a slide (and in the case of images, make sure you have permission to use them!). A single slide at the end with references isn't sufficient.

I know what you're thinking: won't that junk up my gorgeously crafted slide?

It doesn't have to. See how Jonathon Colman references Kristina Halvorson as the originator of an idea in the slide that follows (he also hot-linked it to Kristina's site):

Here's how I gave Doug Kessler at Velocity in London credit for an idea (I also linked to him in the subsequent blog post):

Ideally, you'll cite as you write. It's surprisingly easy to forget what content was your own original work and what you sourced . . . if you let too many hours creep in between the writing and the citing.

This type of memory lapse is actually a thing—psychologist Dan Gilbert calls it *kleptomnesia*, or an accidental plagiarism or belief that an idea you generate is your own when in fact it was someone else's. (A famous example is George Harrison's 1970 hit "My Sweet Lord," which a judge later ruled was accidentally similar in both melody and harmony to a song produced seven years earlier, "He's So Fine" by the Chiffons.)

Having access to millions of sources online is a double-edged sword: it's both liberating and dangerous. Keep careful notes as you research your work, and mark the origin of excerpts of nonoriginal text in the text itself. Keep in mind that many online tools can instantly crawl through millions of records to see whether your writing is actually yours. (See Part VI.)

One final word on citation: you'll notice that, in those two presentation examples I gave, what's cited is actually the source of inspiration for an idea, not the source of the specific idea itself. Calling out the valuable contributions of others, even if it's just inspiration, isn't just a good business practice. It's a good practice, period.

56

Curate Ethically

Content curation is an ugly phrase, isn't it? It suggests the working parts of machinery and implies a kind of automation that takes a blob of colorless fodder, feeds it to a conveyor belt, and plops into a website for mass consumption.

But the truth is that the best kind of content curation has a decidedly human element to it. It might be found, collected, and organized via technology, but its real value materializes when actual people add something new to it: when it's shared with enthusiasm, or it becomes a basis for an expanded opinion or a different take.

If you are merely regurgitating content from elsewhere without adding your take, that's not curation—that's aggregation. A robot can aggregate content, but only a human can tell me why it matters. Your curated content might not be original to you, but you should deliver an original *experience* that adds unique value.

I agree with how Maria Popova writing on BrainPickings.org, views curation:

> *I firmly believe that the ethos at its core—a drive to find the interesting, meaningful, and relevant amidst the vast maze of overabundant information, creating a framework for what matters in the world and why—is an increasingly valuable form of creative and intellectual labor, a form of authorship that warrants thought.*[1]

I love that part about "a form of authorship," because it reframes curation not as an add-on or a rip-off or an easy way to fill a Web page or a blog post quota. Instead, it respects curation as an important, foundational piece of any content marketing program.

More and more companies are using curation. Research from Curata (a content curation technology company) found that although companies are creating most of the content they produce, they are curating nearly a quarter of it.[2]

Content Mix: Created, Curated, Syndicated

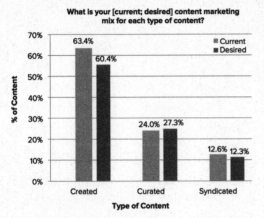

Source: Reproduced by permission of Curata.

Content curation can be a valuable supplement to your publishing program. But bad curation can damage your brand's credibility and potentially lead to copyright and legal issues.

Here's a stern smackdown for anyone who needs it: *taking someone else's content and pasting it as your own into a post is terrible curation, because you effectively steal all of the search engine benefit, traffic, and credit from the original creator.*

Don't do that—even inadvertently. Mentioning the original author in the post is not enough. Verizon ran an entire article that Kerry O'Shea Gorgone had written as a paid columnist for Mark Schaefer's blog, {grow}, but credited neither Kerry nor Mark. Mark wrote a post about the experience on his high-traffic blog, and Verizon came off as a sloppy curator (at best) or a copyright infringer (at worst). How much goodwill did Verizon lose because it didn't bother to cite and link?

Here's how to curate ethically (and well):

◆ **Rely on a variety of sources.** Relying on one or two curation sources isn't just boring for your readers, "it also violates the spirit of good curation because it could well mean you're profiting off of the original creator's work," writes Pawan Deshpande, CEO of Curata, in an article at MarketingProfs.[3]

♦ **Credit the original source (not the secondary).** We talked about this already, but to reiterate: if someone else has created valuable content that benefits your audience, she's doing you a favor, right? Do her a solid in return and help her achieve the recognition and search engine boost she's earned.

♦ **Say it loud and proud.** Cite attribution front and center. Don't be one of those unscrupulous sneaks who bury links at the bottom of a post, disguise links in the same color font as the rest of the article, or use a minuscule font. That doesn't mean you need to swing too far in the other direction and use a 1990s flashing font to highlight attribution. Just link to it conversationally.

The sections you create in your own words should be longer than any sections you're quoting. Quote short passages or a short section of the original piece only—don't reprint the whole enchilada. You're curating parts, not reprinting the whole. The idea is to give your readers the gist of another piece so you can share your take on why it matters, or why it's important, or what else to consider. Extensive quoting will also blur the line between fair use and copyright infringement, says Pawan. (See Rules 57 and 58.)

♦ **Add context and point of view.** Forget about the law for a minute and consider what you're supposed to be doing here to begin with: telling your readers why it matters to them. So, as I noted earlier, add relevant context and value, and (possibly) brand-appropriate keywords that may not have appeared in the original.

♦ **Write a new headline.** You'll want to anyway, to reflect your spin on the topic. But it's also a good idea to further differentiate your piece from the original.

♦ **Avoid nofollow links.** Using nofollow links when citing a source robs the original content creator of some search benefit, so you might prefer to avoid using them.

The nofollow issue, though, does highlight the importance of providing enough information about the author and the work that someone could easily find it if the original link breaks. Links can change, so make every effort to help people find the original source of curated content if they need to.

For example, if I were linking to an article on marketer Mack Collier's site, I'd link his name to his main URL at MackCollier.com, and I'd separately link to the curated article as well. Even if in the future he moves content around, he likely won't change or lose his domain name. So a reader could still click on Mack's name, arrive on his site, and search for the article there.

57

Seek Permission, Not Forgiveness

I've sometimes advocated an approach to life in which I seek forgiveness, not permission, for transgressions. Ignoring copyright isn't one of those times.

Copyright infringement is like smoking marijuana: people tend to think that because it's common it must be legal. It isn't. My analogy is falling apart a bit because of you, Colorado, but here's the bottom line: using other people's copyrighted work in your marketing is not cool.

In other words, in matters of copyright, seek permission, not forgiveness.

Getting permission often boils down to these three steps:

1. *Ask.* You'd be surprised at how often just asking works, but make sure that you're asking the correct person or company for permission. Ownership of copyrighted works can get confusing, particularly in the case of sound recordings and other works in which multiple parties may have a stake.
2. *Get permission in writing.* Some people forget conversations, others may outright lie if there's a large amount of money at stake. Even if the written permission is just in the form of an email, it works. Go beyond a phone call or an in-person conversation.

3. *Honor the terms.* If you receive permission to use someone's song as your podcast introduction, don't assume it's OK to use it for a TV commercial too. The permission will be specific to the proposed use.

View permission requests as an opportunity to build relationships: people will appreciate that you admire their work, which is a great way to begin a conversation. Talking with other content creators in your industry builds your network, and it can lead to partnerships and connections. None of those relationships can develop if you use the other person's work without permission.

A word about images . . . we've been talking mostly about text here, of course. But graphical content, such as infographics, photos, images, and so on, is all subject to copyright law and requires permission for reuse. If that's not an option, find royalty-free images to use, or purchase stock images. (See suggestions for sourcing photos that aren't ho-hum—in other words, stock photos that don't look like stock photos!—in Part VI.)

You can also find images released under a Creative Commons license (http://creativecommons.org/licenses); use Flickr or Google's advanced search option to find them. Also, check for unauthorized image licensing issues using TinEye's reverse image search engine or via Google at http://bit.ly/GoogleSearchImages.

The safest course of action is to always use your own text, images, video, and other content, because you know where it came from. I generally use my own Instagram images on my blog, for example.

I like how the wool clothing company Ibex uses employees as some of its models. The following graphic is its 404 page (ibex.com/404). That's Brian on the left (he has since left the company); J.R., on the right, is an Ibex analyst at the company's White River Junction, Vermont headquarters. They're dancing dressed in Ibex samples that never made it into production, according to Ibex VP of Marketing Keith Anderson.

404 not found

Have you strayed, need a break?
Time for an impromptu dance party!

Dance party over? Return to ibex.com

Unauthorized Use of Your Own Content

What if you discover unauthorized use of your content? Here are steps to take:

1. If a site is using your content without permission, send the site owner a written correspondence (email or letter) letting him or her know you've discovered the use and that you'd like it taken down. (Or that you'd like credit and/or a link back, if that's sufficient for you. Your call.) In many instances people don't realize that they've done something illegal. Some people think a writer is simply flattered to have his or her content used. Weird. But true.

2. If the owner doesn't respond or take action, your next step is to have an attorney draft a cease-and-desist letter that explains the law of copyright as it applies to your work on the site, and explaining the potential legal penalties for not respecting your intellectual property.

3. If the owner ignores your attorney's letter, you have a few options: (1) litigation (expensive and time consuming); (2) contacting the host company of the infringing website and detailing the transgression; or (3) reporting the site to Google for copyright infringement. Getting someone's site de-indexed by Google can be more effective than the threat of a lawsuit. See details on how to report a site to Google at http://bit.ly/GoogleLegalHelp.

Similarly, you can report infringing social media posts to each social network.

Source: These three steps are from Kerry O'Shea Gorgone.

58

Understand the Basics of Copyright, Fair Use, and For Attribution

Sometimes you need to call in the experts. I did that here with Kerry O'Shea Gorgone, who works at MarketingProfs and is also an attorney. (Even so, keep in mind that what follows shouldn't be considered legal advice, which only your attorney can give you.)

ANN HANDLEY: What's the difference between *copyright, fair use,* and *for attribution?*

KERRY O'SHEA GORGONE: *Copyright* is actually a bundle of rights held by the owner of a creative work. For example, if I write a book, I alone hold the right to reproduce it and distribute copies, publish the book, perform or display it publicly, or create derivative works based on it.

Fair use is a *legal defense* against a claim of copyright infringement. The most important thing to realize about fair use is that it won't prevent you from being sued: you only raise the defense once you're already involved in litigation.

The court in a copyright infringement case uses four factors to decide whether your use of the copyrighted work is fair:

1. The purpose and character of the use, including whether such use is of commercial nature or is for nonprofit educational purposes.
2. The nature of the copyrighted work.
3. The amount and substantiality of the portion used in relation to the copyrighted work as a whole.

4. The effect of the use upon the potential market for, or value of, the copyrighted work.

Figuring out which uses are fair from a legal standpoint can be tricky, and ultimately your best guess might be wrong. That's why brands should err on the side of caution and get express, written permission before using someone else's content for marketing.

For attribution allows use with credit to the author or creator of the work. It's ethical (and nice) to provide attribution, but it will not protect you from a claim of copyright infringement, unless the author of the original work released it under a Creative Commons license. These types of licenses permit the free use of creative works, provided certain conditions are met. Different license types have different restrictions. The least restrictive is an Attribution license, meaning you may use the work so long as you credit the original author.

Can I Just Link?

AH: What about reprinting online content in an offline publication? Or quoting in social media—say, on Facebook? Do I need to let the author know or seek permission or can I simply link to the original source?

KOG: Any time you reproduce content in its entirety (or even reproduce a large portion of it), you should get permission.

When quoting in social media, so long as the quote is accurate and doesn't amount to a huge portion of the original work, you should be okay if you cite and link to the original source.

If you can't link to the original source (for example, if the source is an out-of-print book), provide all the information you possibly can so that your readers can find the book. Also, avoid using too much of the source information in your own post. In this instance, I'd probably make an effort to include details like full title, publication date, and publisher.

Always ask for permission before reproducing someone's content (online or offline), because fair use is nearly impossible to determine in advance of a lawsuit, and because if the owner says yes (gives you permission) you're in the clear. (Do get permission in writing, however. Memories fade and a verbal okay may not be enough to clarify the terms of your use.)

What about Images?

KOG: It can sometimes be risky to use a photo that you find tagged with a Creative Commons license (http://creativecommons.org/licenses) because it's possible that the person who posted it was not the copyright holder. Google offers a reverse image look-up, which can be helpful if you want to make sure that the original owner of a photo you want to use has in fact released the rights (http://www.google .com/insidesearch/features/images/searchbyimage.html).

Copyright applies to all different kinds of creative works (musical compositions, motion pictures, works of literature, paintings, sculptures, etc.). Consequently, most types of content are subject to the same rules. Applying these rules can be tricky, though, because you can't really introduce a photo the way you can a literary work.

You often need to display an entire image to illustrate your point, which is, by definition, reproducing the entire picture. If you must do this, I'd recommend embedding the original creator's Instagram post, tweet, or social update on your website (using the embed code provided by the relevant social platform). That way, all the information and context are available to readers.

I would not upload someone else's image to my website, even with attribution, unless I had express written permission. Given the mushy definition of fair use, it's just not worth the risk.

How about Logos and Screenshots?

KOG: Trademark law protects logos in a way similar to how copyright law protects creative works. You're covered by fair use if you're displaying a logo or trademark for purposes of commentary, comparison, etc., but you must be very careful not to make false or defamatory statements about that brand.

If your content is educational in nature and you are using logos to make a point about effective logo design, or, say, the role color plays in consumer buying behavior, you're less likely to meet an objection from the brand.

By contrast, if you display a company's logo above text that details why the company is irresponsible and how you are a better choice for people who care about the environment, you are more likely to find yourself embroiled in a legal tug-of-war, even if you ultimately prevail in court.

Lawyers generally recommend exercising caution in the use of others' trademarked property, and only using logos or screenshots when it's absolutely necessary to make a point.

One Final Point

I like a final point of advice that Kerry shared as an aside: *Don't be an asshat.*

Taking something that doesn't belong to you? Asshat. Taking credit for someone else's work? Definitely asshat.

Entire sites are devoted to hating on people who have plagiarized or stolen other people's copyrighted works. You don't want to end up on one of them!

59

Ground Content in Data

Data puts your content in context and gives you credibility. Ground your content in facts: data, research, fact-checking, and curating. Your ideas and opinions and anecdotes might be part of that story—or they might not be, depending on what you are trying to convey. But the more credible content is rooted in something real, not just your own beliefs.

Said another way: data before declaration. If you are going to tell me what you think, give me a solid reason why you think it. What's been said before? What are people on social media saying about it? What evidence supports your point of view or influences your counterpoint?

If research is part of your story, cite reliable sources. Who or what, exactly, is a reliable source will vary based on your industry—in other words, it's a bit of a judgment call. But here are some good examples:

- A major media outlet (the *New York Times*, the *Washington Post*, and the like; such organizations are generally trustworthy because they usually have internal fact-checkers checking their facts)
- Government agencies
- Research reports
- Well-known experts
- Authoritative nongovernmental organizations (Pew Research, for one)

Three Google Data Sources

1. *Google Trends* allows you to see what others have been searching for over time, graph how often a term has been searched for via Google, and pinpoint where those searchers are located (www.google.com/trends). You can also browse searches by date or see the top searches in various categories via its Top Charts tab (www.google.com/trends/topcharts). Its Explore tab lets you see how a search term has trended over time and the direction it's trended in (www.google.com/trends/explore).

2. *Google's Ngram Viewer* is more obscure, but it lets you search and graph words and phrases from a vast number of books that Google has scanned in public libraries to populate its Google Books search engine (https://books.google.com/ngrams). It's a useful (if quirky) tool for finding trends over a much longer time frame than measured in Internet time.

3. *Think with Google* is geared toward marketers and is intended to be a one-stop research hub that aggregates case studies, articles, infographics, interviews, and other things for 14 industries (thinkwithgoogle.com). Its weekly updates make it a good place to poke around for insights, but I wouldn't rely on it solely.

Part V

13 Things Marketers Write

Parts I through IV of this book deliver pretty much everything you need to create the kind of writing that will make you ridiculously proud of yourself.

But because marketers are often tasked with specific kinds of writing, in Part V I've taken up some of the most common writing tasks that land on marketers' desks.

I'd say this section represents the block and tackle of marketing: *if you get these right, you're winning*. But I'm terrible at sports, so I'm a little insecure about that metaphor. Let's just leave it at this: here are some marketing writing fundamentals for things marketers write.

This is the section of the book to turn to when Aaron the CIO asks you to provide a meta description for your site (a meta description gives search engines and site visitors a pithy explanation of what a site is all about).

This is also the section to thumb through when your boss or client insists that she's compelling enough to sustain an hour-long podcast, or when you're wondering whether 10 minutes is too long for most videos (it is), or when you are tasked with heading up a home-page redesign.

So keep this section handy; my hope is that it will make you look decisive and informed when the others in your meeting shuffle papers around the conference table and wait in silence for someone else to answer.

Speaking of thumbs, keep in mind that the guidelines here are, indeed, rules of thumb. There is no one way to write, remember? And there is no one way to write an email or an infographic or an About Us page, either. ("Anyone who says differently is selling something," as the Man in Black tells the Princess Bride.)

You are free to adapt and amend and reject these guidelines as you discover what works for your audience and for you. But at least you have a place to start.

60

The Ideal Length for Blog Posts, Podcast, Facebook Posts, Tweets, and Other Marketing Content

How Long Should a Blog Post Be?

I get this a lot. Maybe you do, too. Clever Chicago-based marketer Andy Crestodina did the research and compiled the length guidelines for 10 common types of content, shown in the following graphic. He compiled most of the data from studies that analyzed the high performers, based largely on search engine preferences and nuances. But there are some handy nuggets in here that relate to human writers and readers, too.

A quick explanation follows the chart, with some sources cited that back up Andy's research results.

If you are looking for more, check out the full monty on Andy's site at OrbitMedia.com (http://bit.ly/IdealAndy).

Ideal Length Guidelines for Everything In Your Marketing	
Blog Posts *(for ranking)*	1,500 words
Email Subject Lines *(for open rates)*	50 characters or less
Line of Text	12 words
Paragraph	4 lines or less
YouTube video *(for views)*	3 to 3.5 minutes
Podcast	22 minutes
Title Tags	55 characters
Meta Description	155 characters *(maximum)*
Facebook Post *(for likes & shares)*	100 -140 characters
Tweets *(for retweets)*	120 -130 characters
Domain Name	8 characters or less

Length Guidelines for 11 Kinds of Content

1. *Blog post.* The ideal length for a search-optimized blog post is 1,500 words. "Google is a research tool," Andy writes. "Longer pages have more opportunities to indicate their relevance. Google sees longer pages as more likely to contain the answer to the searcher's question."

   See: Kevin Espiritu, "How Important is Content Length? Why Data-Driven SEO Trumps Guru Opinions," *serpIQ*, April 26. 2012, http://blog.serpiq .com/how-important-is-content-length-why-data-driven-seo-trumps-guru-opinions.

   That doesn't mean longer content (more than 1,500 words) isn't warranted when the subject requires it. And it doesn't mean shorter posts are worthless. It means only what the research suggests: from a search engine perspective, around 1,500 is optimal. Obviously, you don't want to pad your posts to reach some magic 1,500-word count. But you know that already, because I covered writing rules pretty thoroughly in Parts I and II. Ideally, you want to worry less about blog post length and more about being useful to your audience. If you can be useful in 300 words, go for it!

2. *Email subject lines.* The ideal email subject line has 50 or fewer characters. But these perform only slightly better than longer subject lines (those with more than 50 characters).

See: John Foreman, "This Just In: Subject Line Length Means Absolutely Nothing," *MailChimp*, September 17, 2012, http://blog.mailchimp.com/ this-just-in-subject-line-length-means-absolutelynothing.

3. *Website text line.* The ideal length for a line of text on a website is 12 words. If a line of text is too long, "it takes more work to travel all the way across a long line of text, back and forth, over and over," Andy writes. "Readers are more likely to lose their place. This slows reading rates and comprehension."

See: Patrick J. Lynch and Sarah Horton, *Web Style Guide* 3rd Edition, http://webstyleguide.com.

4. *Paragraph.* The ideal length for a paragraph is between 3 and 4 lines, *maximum.* But as we talked about earlier, even one will do.

See: Your eyeballs. And mine. (I'm kidding. I don't have a specific source for that one. But test it out, if you doubt it. You'll see.)

5. *YouTube video.* The ideal length for a YouTube video is between 3 and 3½ minutes. I'd actually argue for shorter. Andy points out that YouTube is the second most popular search engine, and the percentage of viewers who watch the entire video is a ranking factor for your video.

(*continued*)

(*continued*)

"If it's very long, fewer viewers may watch the entire video," Andy writes, "which could cause it to rank lower."

Your video will therefore be discovered less often via search, and as a consequence it will be less popular and will probably end up eating lunch alone. It will also not get into a good college and it'll end up a miserable failure, dying in squalor in a sad walk-up tenement wearing nothing but boxer shorts and a gravy-stained T-shirt.

See: Clinton Stark, "What's the ideal length for a YouTube video?," *Stark Insider* [and confirmed by Google], February 6, 2013, www.starkinsider.com/2013/02/whats-the-best-youtube-video-length.html.

6. *Podcast.* The ideal length for a podcast is 22 minutes, because that's the length of the average listener attention span. *(Ooh, squirrel!)*

See: Stitcher, www.stitcher.com.

7. *Title tag.* The ideal length for a title tag is 55 characters. The title tag is what becomes your link text—the first line, in large typeface—in Google search results.

See: Dr. Peter J. Meyers, "New Tag Guidelines and Preview Tool," *The Moz Blog,* March 20, 2014, http://moz.com/blog/new-title-tag-guide-lines-preview-tool.

8. *Meta description.* The ideal length for a meta description is 155 characters. Any more, and the description will be truncated. The meta description, like the title tag, shows up in search results; it's the snippet of descriptive text that appears right below the title tag.

See: Andrew Crestodina, "Web Content Checklist: 17 Ways to Publish Better Content," *The Orbiter,* April 2012, www.orbitmedia.com/blog/web-content-checklist-17-ways-to-publish-better-content.

9. *Facebook post.* The ideal length for a Facebook post is between 100 and 140 characters—or about the same length as a tweet.

"Length isn't the only factor, or even the most important factor," Andy wrote. Images, on the other hand, are important, because Facebook posts with graphics get four times as much response as posts without. But after 140 characters of text, response rates nose-dive.

See: "Optimizing Facebook Engagement—Part 3: The Effect of Post Length," *Track Social Blog*, June 25, 2012, http://tracksocial.com/blog/2012/06/optimizing-facebook-engagement-part-3-the-effect-of-post-length/.

10. *Tweet.* The ideal length for a tweet is between 120 and 130 characters. Twitter technically allows for 140, of course. But the ideal length is shorter so that there's a buffer for manual retweeting.

See: Dan Zarrella, "[Infographic] How to Get More Clicks on Twitter," (blog) http://danzarrella.com/infographic-how-to-get-more-clicks-on-twitter.html.

11. *Domain name.* The ideal length for a domain name is 8 characters, mostly because short is easy to remember.

See: Daniel Scocco, "On Domain Names, Size and Quality DOES Matter!," *Daily Blog Tips*, www.dailyblogtips.com/on-domain-names-size-and-quality-does-matter.

61

Writing for Twitter
Dialogue, Not Monologue

More than almost any other social media platform, Twitter is intended for conversation and banter—often with strangers. That means tweets work best as a dialogue, because dialogue establishes rapport and encourages interaction.

For example, you could simply post a news story with a headline and a link to the original source (in this case, Mashable), like this:

> "How One Woman Hid Her Pregnancy from Big Data," http:// mashable.com/2014/04/26/big-data-pregnancy.

Instead, here's how I posted that story this morning as @marketingprofs (I'm also @annhandley on Twitter), because I wanted to give some context to the story. I explained why I liked it and why I considered it worth sharing.

Ann Handley @MarketingProfs · 4h
A great headline (& great reframing of "big data" in human terms): How One
Woman Hid Her Pregnancy from Big Data mashable.com/2014/04/26/big...

🔲 Hide photo   ↰ Reply ⇄ Retweet ★ Favorite ••• More

🔳 Mashable

How One Woman Hid Her Pregnancy From Big Data
By **Mashable** @mashable

View on web

RETWEETS   FAVORITES
13   **8**

7:46 AM - 27 Apr 2014 · Details   Flag media

Earlier in the book I talked about using Donald Murray's filter for news ("What would make your reader turn and say, 'Now listen to this, Ira . . . '?"). For Twitter, I'm suggesting that you be Ira's wife and write a tweet as if you were talking directly to Ira. Even if you, like me, are sometimes representing a company or brand.

In other words, even though you might be talking to strangers on Twitter, you're still talking to people. So write every tweet as you would speak it . . . to your girlfriend, boyfriend, significant other, dog, cat, goldfish swimming in its fishbowl—or whoever you can imagine in the room with you.

Here's what else to consider . . .

- **Establish who you are.** What's your point of view as a business or business professional? What do you stand for and how do you improve your world? We talked about this in Part III, but again: your point of view is your bigger story—your broader perspective—that represents who you are.

  That perspective can help you discern what to share and what conversations to participate in on Twitter (and LinkedIn, Facebook, and the rest). It can also guide your efforts to share a bit of yourself beyond what your business does to give your followers insight into who you are (without getting too personal or political or religious).

- **Tell your bigger story.** You might be the owner of a cupcake truck, but your bigger story can be that you are passionate about locally sourced food or community-centered activism. Or perhaps you're just an advocate of embracing the simple joys in life. It can be anything. What matters is that it be authentic.

  Someone who does this right is my friend Dharmesh Shah, cofounder and CTO of HubSpot in Cambridge, Massachusetts. His broader perspective—his bigger story—is his passion for start-ups, especially those in the software sector. The things he shares on social channels concern his own business, certainly, but they also revolve around advice and resources to help start-ups succeed.

- **Share the why and who, not just the what.** Remember: think dialogue, not monologue. Social sites are often condemned for encouraging banal and useless noise, such as "Eating a burrito for lunch." But they provide a rich opportunity to share updates that offer context or reveal character.

  So rather than posting "Spent the day reading" (boring), try "Spent the day reading David Sedaris's new book. Unplugging after last week's big shipment!"—which provides both context (why you're doing what you're doing) and a sense of your character (who you are).

- **Don't pitch-slap.** Notice how my previous example didn't say, "Spent the day reading David Sedaris's new book. Unplugging after last week's big shipment! Order today: www.dontdothis.com." That's not social sharing—that's a social pitch-slap. Remember, you're building relationships, not running a direct-marketing channel. Lead with your expertise and personality. Share or solve—don't just pitch whatever it is you sell.

♦ **Personalized, not personal.** True, social platforms allow you to showcase the people behind a brand. But there's a fine line between sharing yourself . . . and sharing a little *too much* of yourself, especially if you are tweeting on behalf of your company.

Think of it this way: personalize your company or yourself, but don't get personal. The former means showing that you're a real human being, with actual blood flowing through actual veins—you have a point of view, a personality. The latter means sharing details that are intimate or too specific to you to have relevance for the larger community you are trying to build.

Exactly where that line is varies according to your own brand and that of your company. But here's a broad example: It's one thing to mention feeling under the weather. It's another to say you have an irritating rash in a sensitive spot. (Celebrities often cross the line. If you are a celebrity reading this, feel free to post a photo of said rash as well.)

♦ **Be cautious with automation.** Many tools are available to help you manage and scale your social presence. IFTTT (If This, Then That) automates tasks such as auto-saving Instagram photos to Dropbox or creating a Facebook update when you check in on Foursquare. SocialOomph can schedule tweets or auto-follow those who follow you; dlvr.it and Buffer can help you schedule and auto-post to several platforms at once. For growing companies, these tools can be handy timesavers.

But a word of caution: don't rely too heavily on automation tools. Use them to extend and ease your social media efforts, not supplant them. For example, robosending automated direct messages to greet each new Twitter follower is annoying. (Do you do it? Stop.)

If your followers sense that you are phoning it in, you'll damage the credibility you are trying to build. What's more, such perfunctory, uncommitted practices run counter to the spirit of social networking—which is, after all, inherently about relationships. In social media (and in life, I suppose), true engagement—person to person—trumps technology.

♦ **Use Twitter as a spawning pool for other content.** Author David Meerman Scott (*New Rules of Marketing and PR* and many other books) floats ideas on Twitter to see what gets nibbles.

"I use what I call a 'writing ladder,'" David told me. "If a tweet resonates—it gets a bunch of RTs and *at* replies—then I consider it good blog post fodder. If a blog post resonates, I'll explore it with a riff in a speech and maybe another blog post or two. If a series of posts on the same topic resonates, that's my next book."

David said he developed *Marketing Lessons from the Grateful Dead* (coauthored with HubSpot CEO Brian Halligan), *Real-Time Marketing & PR*, and *Newsjacking* this way.

Other tips:

♦ **Use a clear call to action** if you want your followers to *do* something.
♦ **Don't sacrifice grammar and spelling or use abbreviations** unless you want to seem like a texting 12-year-old.
♦ **Use Bitly to shorten links,** because it offers rich analytics, and short links generate the most retweets.
♦ **Keep your posts below the 120-character level,** per the chart in Rule 60.

Sloppy Social

On average, one in every 179 English words used on Twitter is spelled incorrectly—making it the sloppiest social platform—ahead of Facebook and Google+, according to research from social media monitoring company Brandwatch. (The company analyzed only those three social media platforms.)

Sometimes misspellings are intentional (Soooooooo or LOLZ or YOLO). But sometimes they're not.

These are the most commonly misspelled words on Twitter and Facebook (according to Brandwatch's study of almost 1 million public mentions on the two platforms):

♦ Definitely
♦ Separate

- ◆ Embarrass
- ◆ Achieve
- ◆ Surprise
- ◆ Weird
- ◆ Government
- ◆ Argument

Source: Joel Windels, "Language on the Internet," *Brandwatch*, May 29, 2013, www
.brandwatch.com/2013/05/research-shows-twitter-is-driving-english-language-
evolution.

Here are some other, sometimes hilarious examples of misspellings. Presumably these tweets were posted without intentional typos,
since the originals have been deleted. But they live on as embarrassing
screenshots.

From @ScopeMouthwash (especially surprising because the tweet
was a promoted tweet!):

Source: http://simplysylviesays.blogspot.com/2013/01/spot-mistake.html.

From @GrubStreetNY (now @GrubStreet), a New York food and restaurant blog:

From British Parliament member Andrew Selous:

Source: www.huffingtonpost.co.uk/2013/06/26/andrew-selous-mp-twitter-gaffe-benefits-language-lessons_n_3503267.html.

Typos happen, of course. And keep in mind that a robot spell-checker can't catch all of them.

Consider this alarming blunder in a recipe printed in *The Pasta Bible*, issued by Penguin Australia in 2010: the book recommended seasoning a dish of tagliatelle with sardines and prosciutto with "salt and freshly ground black people," according to a news story in the *Guardian*. No recall was made of the books in circulation, but the publisher destroyed the remaining 7,000 printed copies, at a cost of $20,000.[1]

Content hack: Try reading each sentence backward, instead of the usual way. Doing so jars your brain to consider each word independently, allowing you to spot typos more readily.

62

Writing with Hashtags
(Or, Don't Be a Hash-hole)

Justin Timberlake and Jimmy Fallon mocked the ridiculous overuse of hashtags with a hilarious sketch last fall on Fallon's late-night show. Their "Twitter Conversation in Real Life" was littered with excessive hashtagging (my favorite part, mocking #LOL: *hashtag-el-o-el-o-el-o-el-o-el-o-el-o-el-o-el* . . .). The sketch also skewered what happens when companies—and all of us!—get a little too carried away with tacking a hashtag onto every social media utterance.[1]

TechCrunch's Jordan Crook bluntly referred to people who abuse the hashtag as *hash-holes*, according to Nick Ehrenberg, writing in a post at Top Rank Marketing's blog.[2]

But you know what? Hashtags don't have to be gratuitous and silly. Hashtags can serve a purpose—they can help tell your story, share your history, and align you with an audience.

In social media, the pound symbol (or hash) turns any word (or group of words) that directly follows it into a searchable link or keyword on Twitter, Vine, Facebook, Instagram, Tumblr, Google+, and Pinterest. A hashtag becomes a handy shortcut, a way for people to categorize, find, and rally around topics and conversations. So if you want to chat with others about the new season of *Scandal* on Netflix, you might use and search for #Scandal (and #Olitz, if you're among the obsessed!) to follow the conversation.

Twitter is the birthplace of the hashtag. The platform's conversational, casual nature means that Twitter hashtags tend to be more adaptable (more on that in a minute).

Here are some ways you might consider using and writing hashtags:

- **Share your history.** #ThrowbackThursday (or #tbt) began organically, as a way for people on Instagram to share pictures of themselves as kids, or to reminisce about historical events or occasions. First Lady Michelle Obama (@michelleobama) often uses the popular Thursday meme to post a throwback photo of herself—as a dancer in college, with her brother as a child, in her high school graduation yearbook photo, and so on.

  Similarly, some companies have adopted the weekly ritual as a way to share some of their own brand history. *People* magazine (@peoplemag, with 421K followers) recently celebrated its fortieth birthday by using an Instagram video to flip through the pages of its first issue. Dated March 4, 1974, it featured a dewy Mia Farrow on the cover, photos of a young Prince Charles, and pictures of gymnast Cathy Rigby, who had just retired from her Olympic career.

  I also like the way Toyota posts #tbt on Instagram to not only highlight the longevity of its vehicles but also to place them in historical context. For example, around the Super Bowl in February 2014, Toyota posted a photo of its classic 2000GT with the caption, "In 1967, Americans watched the first 'big game' and this beauty was on the roads." More broadly, Toyota has used the hashtag to align its brand with U.S. history and American values.

- **Tap into what people care about.** The biggest mistake a company can make with hashtags is to assume that people want to talk about its dumb brand. They don't.

  Although sometimes creating a hashtag that includes a brand name can help ground the conversation—giving context and making it self-evident what tweets are referring to (like the #Scandal example I gave earlier in the book), it's generally better to connect with people on social networks by tapping into conversations that are already happening in terms already being used. People want to talk about what matters to *them*—not what matters to *you* as a company, organization, or brand. As Tom Fishburne of Marketoonist.com says, "Brand loyalists are loyal to a brand only as long as a brand complements their own life and priorities."

Sometimes efforts to get people to talk about how awesome you are with a targeted, brand-specific hashtag can backfire—disastrously—as the New York Police Department found out in April 2014. Its outreach campaign to get people to share pictures of themselves posing with police officers and to use the #MyNYPD hashtag ignited a kind of anticampaign, inspiring people nationwide to post photos of police brutality on Twitter and Instagram.

On the other hand, the New York Public Library (@nypl) used hashtags brilliantly in February 2014, when it tweaked the notion of the #selfie and asked book lovers to post "#shelfies" on Twitter and Instagram—that is, photos of personal bookshelves or favorite library shelves, as a way to profess their love of books and celebrate the role books play in our lives. The response was impressive: more than 1,500 people posted on Instagram and 1,800 posted on Twitter. Entries came from 14 countries and 28 U.S. states.

In March, the NYPL did it again (as I noted in Rule 47). Referencing college basketball's March Madness to hold an author smackdown of #literarymarchmadness, the library pitted various authors against one another in various "conferences": Triple Threats (Zora Neale-Hurston versus Edna St. Vincent Millay), Real-Life Feuds (Gabriel Garcia Marquez versus Mario Vargas Llosa), Kid Favorites, Cult Following, and so on. The library's 25,000 Instagram followers voted for their favorites via the comments.

Morgan Holzer, an information architect at the NYPL, launched the program along with Billy Parrott, who runs the library's Art Picture Collection. "Whenever possible, add personality," Morgan suggested when I asked her what other organizations could learn from the library's efforts.

"Followers know there is a person behind the scenes and will get turned off if your post sounds automatic," Morgan said. "We like to use humor on the NYPL's Instagram and people appreciate it. People want to see what you see, not just what they can see."

A more pedestrian (but no less potentially effective) take on this idea of tapping into what people already care about would be to tag your travel deals, for example, with #cheaptravel, or business know-how content with #marketingadvice or #whatImreading, and so on—in other words . . . broader, nonbranded keywords you'd like to be aligned with.

♦ **Convey your personality.** Writing at the *New Yorker* a few years ago, Susan Orlean said hashtags can also function as a kind of "muttered into a handkerchief" aside—that is, purely entertaining commentary conveying deadpan remarks, humor, sarcasm, or context. Hashtags like #kidding and #fail #sorrynotsorry fall into this category. Or, as Susan offers: "I just made out with your husband! #kidding #hewishes #likeIwouldadmititanyway."[3]

Brands using hashtags in this way convey personality through a kind of social voice and tone. We talked about voice and tone in Rule 43, but consider how hashtags can add both to your social posts.

Here are a few good examples:

• Nestlé brand's DiGiorno Pizza live-tweeted commentary during NBC's live broadcast of *The Sound of Music* with Carrie Underwood in December 2013, via #TheSoundofMusicLive on Twitter. One of my favorites (https://twitter.com/DiGiorno Pizza/statuses/408767675838390273):

DiGiorno Pizza ✅   ▼ Follow
@DiGiornoPizza

#TheSoundOfMusicLive **Can't believe pizza isn't one of her favorite things smh**

8:19 PM - 5 Dec 2013

701 RETWEETS **602** FAVORITES

• The legalization of weed sales might be too much a hot potato for most brands to comment on. But, despite being owned by the huge Unilever, Ben & Jerry's playfully commented on the legalization of marijuana in Colorado in January 2014. I only wish Ben & Jerry's had included a hashtag in this tweet, because it was a hilarious bit of social commentary:

 **Ben & Jerry's** ✓   ☼ˇ   Following
@benandjerrys

BREAKING NEWS: We're hearing reports of stores selling out of Ben & Jerry's in Colorado. What's up with that? pic.twitter.com/zBs8nyxZWn

↩ Reply   ♺ Retweet   ★ Favorite   ••• More

RETWEETS   FAVORITES
10,447   6,353

4:02 PM - 2 Jan 2014   Flag media

- And, finally, mobile app TalkTo frequently appends the hashtag #NoMoreCalls to its tweets. It sounds like a rallying cry against robocalls or Alexander Graham Bell, but it's really just a cheeky way to convey some personality and align with its broader story since TalkTo is an app (recently acquired by Path) that allows you to text any company instead of calling it (in other words: no time wasted on hold).

    Those examples are quirky expressions of personality, of stories told through social media and punctuated by hashtags.

Hone your own voice and tone to make them uniquely yours, based on who you are as a brand and how you need to communicate with those you are trying to reach.

Hashtags can help. Consider them your secret sauce in the content brisket.

Here are some other tips:

- **Track and follow trending hashtags** on the various platforms themselves, or via Hashtags.org (www.hashtags.org), which categorizes and gives some details for each.
- **RiteTag** (http://ritetag.com) is a tool that can offer hashtag suggestions for any topic; it can also let you A/B test various alternatives. It has both free and paid options.
- **Don't use more than two or three hashtags** in a social post, especially on Instagram, where #Too #Many #People #Over #Hashtag. I'm talking to you, Trident:

63

Writing Social Media with Humor

Strong Voice, Tight Writing: A Q&A with Tiffany Beveridge, Creator of My Imaginary Well-Dressed Toddler Daughter

Freelance copywriter Tiffany Beveridge created a Pinterest board in early 2012 for a fake daughter and fashion icon she named Quinoa.

Or, more specifically, she created the board to record the ridiculously over-the-top lifestyle and crazy fashion choices of the fictitious Quinoa and her imaginary daughter's imaginary fashion-forward friends—people she named Houndstooth, Hashtag, Boursin, Amino, and especially Quinoa's BFF Chevron.

She called the Pinterest board My Imaginary Well-Dressed Toddler Daughter (MIWDTD) (www.pinterest.com/tiffanywbwg/my-imaginary-well-dressed-toddler-daughter). It pairs over-the-top photos of trendy models (wearing haute couture and aloof expressions) with hilarious captions.

The board has blown up on the interwebs—growing its follower base from its initial follower count of around 100 to more than 90,000 as of the spring of 2014—earning Tiffany press coverage and, eventually, a book deal. Running Press published *How to Quinoa: Life Lessons from My Imaginary Well-Dressed Daughter* in June 2013.

If there's a more entertaining board on Pinterest, I don't know what it is. One of the reasons I love Quinoa's board is that it's a fun take on the over-the-top consumerism of Pinterest. If I were a sociologist, I might suggest that MIWDTD is a kind of postmodernist commentary on a consumer-driven society punctuated with the inevitable longing for flawless, flaxen-haired, coifed and polished offspring. I'm not a sociologist, so I'd say I like it just because, you know, it's fun.

But at the same time it's an interesting look at how a strong voice and tight writing on social media can singlehandedly transform a presence from *meh* to marvelous. I asked Tiffany to share her perspective on writing for social media, how humor comes from the unexpected, and what she does when the words just don't come.

ANN HANDLEY: You have two sons. What gave you the inspiration for the MIWDTD?

TIFFANY BEVERIDGE: My two sons couldn't care less what they wear. It's a constant parade of T-shirts and basketball shorts around here.

I kept seeing cute things on Pinterest for girls on my feed, but felt I had no claim to them. Then I thought, why not? Why can't I pin cute stuff for girls? So I named the board for my imaginary daughter and started repinning clothes from friends that I thought were cute and fun.

When I started searching for little girl clothes on Pinterest myself . . . I discovered the over-the-top photos and looks. And then I guess my sense of humor got the better of me. I mean, come on, if I'm going to spend time dressing an imaginary daughter on Pinterest, why not go all the way?

AH: The board is hilarious. But the more recent stuff is funnier. When I read your early entries you definitely seemed to be still finding your voice. This isn't really a question. It's just an observation, I guess.

TB: You're exactly right. The whole look and persona of Quinoa has definitely evolved. She used to be much more altruistic. Now she just *thinks* she is.

AH: What's your general advice about writing for social media?

TB: Having spent many years as a copywriter, I have learned three helpful skills:

1. Always try to say it again in fewer words.
2. Trust your own voice.
3. Use humor whenever possible.

Especially [in] social media, there is so much content out there, so much noise, and I think we have trained ourselves to scour information at a lightning-fast pace. If you have a clear, concise idea that has an authentic voice, it helps to set you apart.

And humor (especially in writing) is a fairly rare commodity, so if you've got it, use it. After all, who doesn't like to laugh? Think

about your favorite Super Bowl commercials in the past. Chances
are, the ones you remember best were funny.

AH: How do you approach your writing there? Can you give us some
insight to your process?

TB: I try to tell the most story in the fewest words. I study the photos
and make sure that I'm including everything I can about what is
available in the frame, and then I try to think of an unexpected
context for the scene.

One time I was working on a pin that showed a girl in a room
with a flamingo and fake snow all over the floor. I was a bit
stumped. My 10-year-old son was walking by my desk and I
stopped him and asked, "If that isn't snow on the ground in that
picture, what could it be?" Without missing a beat, he said, "Parmesan cheese."

I go back to that experience a lot. It could have been a funny
pin if I'd included snow in the caption, but it became hilarious when
suddenly it was Parmesan cheese on the floor.

AH: So the photo becomes the visual punch line.

TB: Yes. Always go for the unexpected.

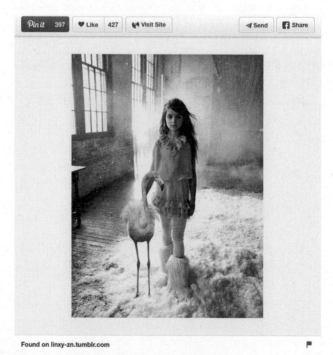

Found on linxy-zn.tumblr.com

Source: Used with permission of Cleo Sullivan.

AH: Do you think about it a lot, or do things just come to you?

TB: The process is usually very quick, about 15 minutes or so. That's how it's been from the beginning, so I've tried not to mess with the process too much. I've always been a fast writer and a subscriber of Natalie Goldberg's *Writing Down the Bones* method of burning through to your "first thoughts" with speed. I write out a sentence, then I see if I can tighten it or shorten it. Then I read it out loud to test the cadence and make sure the punch line hits at the right place. Sometimes I'll do a little bit more tweaking, then I hit *Pin it* and let it go.

   I have found that if the process is taking too long, say more than 30–45 minutes, I'm in trouble and I try to put it away for a while. Forcing the funny never works for me. It's like the joke isn't ripe yet and I've got to let my subconscious spend some time getting it soft and sweet.

AH: What role does your audience play? Do you consider them?

TB: I do think about the audience. They have become such a fun part of the story, and they demand excellence, which keeps me on my toes. If I neglect a detail, there is almost always a comment that points it out. They seem to know the character as well as I do, and their comments are often as funny as, if not funnier than the original caption.

   I am so flattered that they get the joke and enjoy it so much. And I never forget that without them, I would never have had the opportunity to write a book.

64

Writing for Facebook
Rallying Cries That Unite an Audience

Company posts on Facebook used to reach approximately 16 percent of their fans. As I'm writing this in the spring of 2014, that number is a puny 2.5 percent because of changes Facebook introduced in December 2013 to its News Feed algorithm.

That's been sobering for a lot of companies who previously built large followings and had decent engagement on Facebook, because it means that marketers now have to pay—that is, buy ads—for the same reach they used to get for free. To many companies, it feels a bit like a shakedown. But Facebook is, after all, a business run by Mark Zuckerberg—not an almshouse run by Mother Teresa.

So is it worth building a fan presence there? That's a question you can only answer in the context of your larger digital strategy—but in any case, it does mean that your Facebook content isn't getting any *less* important.

In April 2013, friends Corey O'Loughlin and Nina Vitalino launched Prep Obsessed, (facebook.com/prepobsessed), their store on Facebook. In June of 2014, they recorded $83,000 in retail sales, and they are on track to record $1 million in sales in the next year, with a healthy profit margin.

Part of their success is attributable to their content marketing and community-building efforts, so it's worth deconstructing their approach to their content and strategy to derive some broader lessons. Your own business might be very different from Prep Obsessed's retail site, of course. But almost any of us can learn something from its approach:

- **Connect with existing communities of potential buyers.** In Prep Obsessed's case, Nina and Corey connected with communities of preppy women on Facebook before launching their business.
- **Target by niche, not numbers.** With the enormous amount of demographic and behavioral information it has on its users, Facebook makes it relatively easy to target your audience according to specific interests. The key to success, then, is being very clear about who your potential customer is—to think niche, not number of Likes.

   Prep Obsessed targets a relatively narrow profile of user: women in the United States who are between 20 and 50 in age and who have expressed an interest in specific retail brands and specific categories. It also targets the friends of its existing fans.
- **Remember that Facebook isn't free.** Facebook isn't a free network—it's only a free *platform.* That means you'll need to have a marketing budget.

   Prep Obsessed spends $40 a day on Facebook ads, or $15,000 annually. That seems like a lot. But it's paid off: over the course of nine months, that strategy has netted the fledgling company more than 55,000 fans, with the cost of acquisition less than 10 cents each. And it's a highly engaged audience.
- **Unite an audience with rallying cries.** Prep Obsessed's growth rate of 600–700 fans a day isn't just due to advertising. Two-thirds of its fans come organically, via awareness generated by content posted on its page—mostly the Words to Live By quotes and images that Corey describes as "rallying cries that unite the audience."

   For example, a recent quote from *Gossip Girl* character (and preppy icon) Blair Waldorf netted more than 400 likes and 99 shares, further spreading awareness of Prep Obsessed:

Words to Live By: Preppy Quotables

Back to Album · Prep Obsessed's Photos · Prep Obsessed's Page   Previous · Next

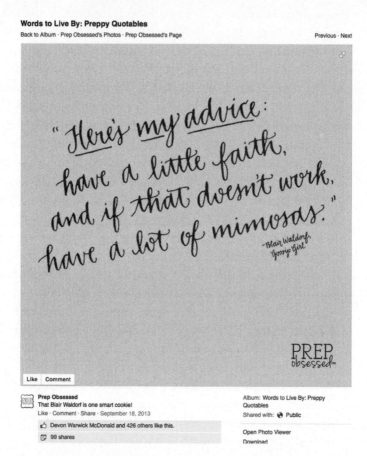

Like   Comment

Prep Obsessed
That Blair Waldorf is one smart cookie!
Like · Comment · Share · September 18, 2013

👍 Devon Warwick McDonald and 426 others like this.

🔄 99 shares

Album: Words to Live By: Preppy
Quotables

Shared with: 🌐 Public

Open Photo Viewer
Download

The brand's online voice and tone are important. Posts and other communication address the audience as *ladies*, because it suggests a gentility and refinement this audience connects with. Corey and Nina sign each email or Facebook post with *xo*, because it suggests friendship and intimacy.

Also, because Prep Obsessed seeks to be an authority and a resource for a certain kind of woman who looks to it to curate the best in preppy accessories, housewares, and gifts, "we never ask what [our customers] want us to offer them," Corey says. "Instead, they are confident that we know what they want because they're confident we love the same things."

Other tips:

- **Post when your audience is online.** Post when your audience is there, not just when your business is open. Facebook users engage with brands more on Fridays than on other days of the week, according to a recent report from Adobe that looked at 260 billion Facebook ad impressions and 226 billion Facebook post impressions from the first quarter of 2014. Some 15.7 percent of all impressions in the quarter occurred on a Friday—the most of any day. Thursday had the second highest share of impressions (14.5 percent), and Sunday had the lowest share (13.4 percent).[1]
- **Posts with images get the highest amount of engagement on Facebook.** Graphics are good; the perfect size is 800 × 600 pixels. Video does well, too: engagement with video posts in the first quarter of 2014 was up 25 percent year over year, and 58 percent quarter over quarter, according to the Adobe report.
- **Keep it brief.** Limit posts to 100–140 characters, as explained in the chart included in Rule 60.

65

Writing for LinkedIn

Always Be Helping

It thrills me to see LinkedIn gaining ground as an interesting place to hang out. I've long held that LinkedIn is the dark horse of the social media platforms—or, at least, it's the workhorse of the bunch. If Twitter is where you go to meet people you don't know and Facebook is where you go to talk with people you do know, then LinkedIn is where all of you can meet up to get stuff done together.

LinkedIn's effort to become a daily content destination is transforming it from merely a digital Rolodex to something inherently more valuable and more interesting. In addition to the site's individual profiles, businesses can also maintain Company pages, follow influencers, access news and updates via the mobile app Pulse, and create Showcase pages to highlight company brands, products, and services.

It's a busy place. So how can marketers best take advantage of LinkedIn's expanded offerings? I asked Jason Miller, LinkedIn's senior director of content marketing, how marketers can best create content there.

ANN HANDLEY: Everyone on LinkedIn should have . . . what?
JASON MILLER: Three things:

1. *An optimized profile.* Keyword-rich descriptions, standout headline, link-backs to blogs, Twitter handle, and (most importantly), a profile that is actively sharing relevant content on a

consistent basis. It's not only great for building a personal brand, it's a fantastic way to increase organic reach for a company's most important content.

2. *A robust company page.* First and foremost make sure your company page is accurate and has a complete description. Next add a compelling banner and be sure to be actively sharing relevant content.

3. *A habit to curate useful news or insights via company pages.* There are several ways to effectively curate useful content for a Company page. From following influencers to diving into Pulse each morning to following relevant companies and other thought leaders, it's easy to find, curate, and share relevant content.

AH: What are tips or tricks you'd suggest to make each more effective?

JM: Be consistent and track your results. Find out what's working from your Company page analytics and scale your efforts with Sponsored Updates.

And don't forget about your employees; empowering them to share news and updates and teaching them how to optimize their profile can have a significant impact on both awareness and lead gen.

AH: Is it better to share content as an individual or through a Company page?

JM: The short answer is both. While I think that the Company page is the hub for your company messaging, encouraging employees to share relevant updates with their network is a very powerful way to increase both reach and engagement.

AH: What time should you post, and how often? Any advice?

JM: Based on my own experience with managing Company pages and Showcase pages, I would recommend three to five times per day. If you have an international presence, then I would also recommend targeted messages overnight as well. Once you find the messages that are resonating, try running a Sponsored Update to reach beyond your initial following.

Consider which segment your target consumers are likely to fall into and plan the timing of your company updates accordingly. For example, if your target audience works in highly regulated or scheduled environments that make it hard for them to read while at work (e.g., finance or health care industries), try posting company updates in the morning, evening, and on the weekend. If they are likely to commute on public transportation (e.g., professionals who live in New York City, Chicago, etc.), try posting during morning and evening commute times.

AH: As LinkedIn has become more of a content platform than just a mere digital Rolodex, what specific kind of company updates or posts drive the most interest and engagement there? News head-lines? Or more general how-to or industry updates?

JM: It's all about the content, and more specifically professional content. We have observed that professionals act very differently on a professional social network; in addition, they consume content differently while on LinkedIn.

People spend time on other social networks, but they *invest* time in LinkedIn. In fact, content pages on LinkedIn receive seven times the views compared with job activity. Our members are seeking professional content that inspires, educates, and ultimately helps them be great at what they do.

The companies and brands that are finding success are doing so by mixing it up. It's going to take a bit of trial and error to see what resonates with your audience, but once you do find the types of posts that work well for your brand, it's time to scale by using Sponsored Updates. I think the most important thing to keep in mind is to not only talk about your company or brand, but instead share content that is helpful and ties back to what your product or service does.

Change your mind-set from "always be closing" to "always be helping." This is a great place to build relationships with an audience and earn their trust.

AH: Do different kinds of updates work for Sponsored Updates? Or does that just give engaging posts a needed boost?

JM: It really depends on your business goals and marketing objectives. Sponsored Updates are very effective for driving leads, brand awareness, event registration, and thought leadership. Once you have defined your goals, then try posting content to your page and optimize your messaging for the best results. Here are a few tips for driving results:

- ◆ Optimize introductions and headlines and add your point of view.
- ◆ Think like a journalist by using concise intros and snappy headlines for higher conversion.
- ◆ Always include a clear call to action, such as a link.
- ◆ Include an image or some type of rich media. Images generally result in an 89 percent higher comment rate.
- ◆ Align content to your member's needs and interests.
- ◆ Make your content snackable and valuable.
- ◆ Manage your updates by measuring engagement and following up on comments.

AH: Your page should *"tell a story . . ."*—yeah, yeah. So who does this really well?

JM: There are lots of examples of companies that are telling their story well with LinkedIn Company pages, both business-to-business and business-to-consumer. One example that comes to mind for B2B is Adobe and the way they use their Company page and Showcase page to tell the story around their multiple product lines with compelling content and great visuals:

Adobe #Adobe Originals turns 25, and we're celebrating with the release of our 100th #typeface - free to you - and a look back at our typographic history: http://adobe.ly/Type25.

Good typography is something everyone sees but no one notices.

John Warnock
ADOBE CO-FOUNDER

ADOBE ORIGINALS | 25 years of original typeface design
100 typeface families
http://adobe.ly/Type25

Like (295) · Comment (4) · Share · 1 day ago

Cindy Mines, Kevin Wolff +293

A great example of B2C is Secret deodorant's Showcase page and how they take the theme of confidence in the workplace and weave it throughout their content to drive awareness and engagement.

AH: Deodorant? Really?

JM: Yeah. B2C is an emerging category here.

AH: Do you think effective writing on LinkedIn updates is different from writing on any other social network—in approach, say? Or are the *rules* different there?

JM: I think there are certainly some differences. For example, when writing your updates on LinkedIn, it's important to keep in mind which audience you are targeting. Is your message crafted to reach the C-suites, the director-level marketers, managers, etc.? With the targeting capabilities on LinkedIn, there is a great opportunity to cater your messaging to a certain audience for better engagement.

66

Writing Your LinkedIn Profile

'Responsible' Is Overrated

Would you say that you are "a strategic, driven expert responsible for innovative and effective programs across the organization"?

Ick. I hope not. But if you did, you'd sound like a million other professionals (literally!) on LinkedIn—which, with more than 300 million members, is the world's largest professional network.[1]

We talked about using words that best describe *you*, and not just the words that could describe anyone else, in Parts II and III of this book. And that means being more intentional with the words you use everywhere—in your social media bios, and also on your LinkedIn profile.

Each year for the past four, LinkedIn has released a list of the top buzzwords and phrases culled from LinkedIn member profiles. Globally, the current most overused buzzword in LinkedIn Profiles is *responsible*, according to LinkedIn. It was used twice as many times as any other word on the list.

The 2013 list is shown in the graphic that follows:

Here are this year's top 10 most overused buzzwords. How many times do these words show up in your profile?

(1)	*responsible*	(6)	*expert*
(2)	*strategic*	(7)	*organizational*
(3)	*creative*	(8)	*driven*
(4)	*effective*	(9)	*innovative*
(5)	*patient*	(10)	*analytical*

Don't sound like everyone else. Find words that differentiate you from others, and then tie those attributes of yours that the words describe to tangible examples. As LinkedIn's career expert, Nicole Williams, explains:

> *Differentiate yourself by uniquely describing what you have accomplished . . . and back it up with concrete examples of your work by adding photos, videos, and presentations to your LinkedIn Profile that demonstrate your best work. Providing concrete examples to illustrate how you are responsible or strategic is always better than just simply using the words.*[2]

Here are two other suggestions from Nicole:

1. *Use active language, citing tangible outcomes.* Be specific about what you've done, and use active language to describe your accomplishments. Instead of saying you are "responsible for content marketing programs," you might say you "increased blog subscribers 70 percent over three years, resulting in a 15 percent increase in leads generated and a 30 percent decrease in the average length of a sale."

   Or, instead of saying you are "responsible for chucking wood," you might say you "hit the quarterly goal of chucking more wood than a woodchuck chucks if a woodchuck could chuck wood."

2. *Mirror the language of the companies you want to work for.* Nicole suggests job candidates tailor their profiles on LinkedIn by selecting the right words for specific opportunities based on an aspirational role in a company you'd like to work for. One of the best ways of standing out, she said, is to mirror the language of the organization you're applying to.

"Follow the company you want to work for on LinkedIn and you'll not only discover what their business goals and priorities are, but also the words and phrases they use to describe these objectives," Nicole suggested in an email interview.

"Companies want to hire people who have an understanding of who they are and what they do," Nicole says. "If you already sound like them they'll be more apt to reach out to you if you're already talking their talk."

In other words: go to the source and adopt its language. Of course, that approach applies whether or not you're looking for a job. Your profile should complement the content marketing you engage in via LinkedIn; it should, like your content, appeal to a specific target audience or industry by using their vocabulary.

Other tips:

- ♦ **Claim your LinkedIn vanity URL,** which makes your profile look more memorable and professional, and makes it easier to share.
- ♦ **Consider the key words you want to be known for,** and optimize your profile by including those words in your headline and summary.
- ♦ **Customize your profile** rather than using the LinkedIn defaults. The LinkedIn profile format is a standard template, of course. But you *can* move parts around, embed examples or other media, and include descriptive headlines.

If you're stuck for headline inspiration, LinkedIn itself can give you some ideas, suggests salesperson Tobias Schremmer from Austin, Texas, who works with me at MarketingProfs.

"If you are in edit mode on your profile, LinkedIn helpfully adds two options: *Show examples* and *See what others in your industry are using*," Tobias said. Dig around for some ideas, and then use them to inspire your own original headline.[3]

Get more specific advice on customizing and optimizing your profile at http://help.linkedin.com.

Chapter **67**

Writing for Email
What Would You Open (WWYO)?

People on your email list have asked to receive your emails—at least, I hope they have (you are using an opt-in list, right?). (See the second-to-last paragraph of this rule.) That's an advantage: you have the privilege of interacting with a person by invitation, in the relatively intimate setting of the recipient's own in-box.

Considering the volume of marketing email being sent, its projected growth, and (too often) pitiful open rates, I suspect many of us are doing it wrong. Many still treat email as a broadcast tactic—using a word like *blast* to describe an email campaign, or not segmenting a list to make messages relevant to the people who care the most, or not testing various approaches to see what works with their audience.

In other words: this is a good time to rethink your email content, to reconsider what you're sending, and why, and how you're communicating. Earlier we talked about swapping places with your reader. Here, I'm suggesting you swap places with your recipient and write an email *you* would open.

Much of the typical advice around email marketing writing is straightforward:

- ◆ **Use short subject lines.** Emails with subject lines of 6–10 words have the highest open rates, yet most emails sent by marketers have subject lines of 11–15 words, according to a

March 2014 report from Retention Science, which looked at 260 million delivered emails and 540 campaigns. (As noted in Rule 60, MailChimp suggests something similar—50 characters total.)

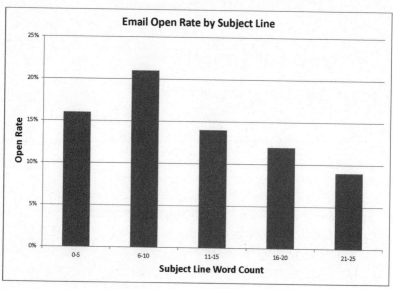

Source: Retention Science.

- ♦ **Let your free flag fly.** Marketers used to be cautioned to avoid using words in the subject line that would trigger a spam filter, like *free* or *lifetime* (or *fast Viagra delivery*). With ISPs relying on advanced filtering and authentication, the specific words used in subject lines are now less worrisome, according to Carolyn Nye, writing in PracticalEcommerce. But there are exceptions, "even now, depending on the ISP," she wrote. Avoid:

    Excessive use of punctuation and capitalization, such as a ! and a ? in the same subject line

    Using a $ sign at the beginning of the subject line

    Misleading subject lines with false promises (of course)[1]

- ♦ **Use the recipient's first name.** Emails with the recipient's first name in the subject line had a higher open rate (18.3 percent compared with 15.7 percent) than those without the name, according to the Retention Science report.

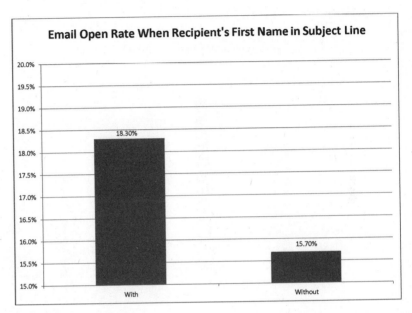

Source: Retention Science.

- ◆ **Keep email copy short.** As with any content, brevity usually rules. (More on that in a minute.) In most cases you should get to the point right away, because most of your readers are probably viewing their email on a mobile device with a limited screen view. (In the fourth quarter of 2013, 55 percent of email opens and 37 percent of clicks took place on a mobile device.)[2] What's missing from the typical roundup of email-related advice is a focus on the content itself—and the need for a personal approach.
- ◆ **Be a real person.** Write with a point of view—from an actual person to an actual person. I don't necessarily mean this literally. The *from* line might still be the company's brand name, but the content should *feel* as if it comes from an actual person, speaking to me in the first person (using *I* or *we* and *you*), with natural-sounding language.

A good example is the following email, from TaskRabbit, sent from the company's name (not a person's). It nonetheless oozes with the kind of approach I'm advocating.

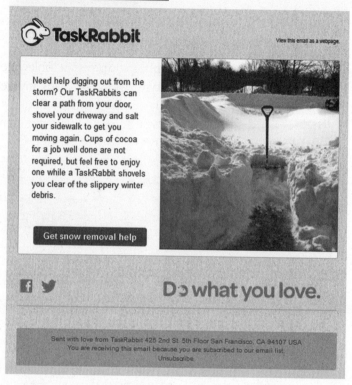

From: TaskRabbit <no-reply@taskrabbit.com>
Date: February 13, 2014 10:25:00 AM EST
To: Ann <ann@marketingprofs.com>
Subject: **Enough with the snow already**
Reply-To: TaskRabbit <no-reply@taskrabbit.com>

TaskRabbit   View this email as a webpage.

Need help digging out from the storm? Our TaskRabbits can clear a path from your door, shovel your driveway and salt your sidewalk to get you moving again. Cups of cocoa for a job well done are not required, but feel free to enjoy one while a TaskRabbit shovels you clear of the slippery winter debris.

Get snow removal help

Do what you love.

Sent with love from TaskRabbit 425 2nd St. 5th Floor San Francisco, CA 94107 USA
You are receiving this email because you are subscribed to our email list.
Unsubscribe.

Why does it work?

- **Context.** This email is timely, having arrived in my in-box on February 13, after another greater-Boston snowstorm had left my own driveway looking pretty much like the one in the photo.
- **It has enormous empathy.** I opened it because *heck yeah . . . enough is enough!* The copy, too, appeals to me on a purely emotional level: Did I almost cry when I woke up to 20 inches of fresh powder and a car buried somewhere under the drifts? Yes, I did. In its email, TaskRabbit under-stands, saying: Relax. We've got this.

- **It communicates with a human voice.** Your choice of email voice is related to the previous point about empathy. TaskRabbit doesn't speak in a generic, formal manner—as in "Another winter storm has delivered 20 inches of snow to greater Boston's doorstep. TaskRabbit clears the snow so homeowners don't have to." It uses *you* and *your* repeatedly, which makes it clear that the email isn't about TaskRabbit, it's about me—how TaskRabbit can help me. Subtle difference (maybe), but a critical one (definitely).

- **It uses real images.** Stock photography that looks like stock photography is so yesterday. TaskRabbit uses images that almost look like they've been snapped with someone's smart phone. When it's possible, you might consider punctuating emails with images from your Instagram or Pinterest feeds, or using photos taken by your staff.

- **It has a specific call to action.** The giant orange box says *Get snow removal help.* It doesn't generically say *Call us* or *Get in touch.* I like how Joanna Wiebe of Copyhackers.com described this approach when she said (at Authority Intensive 2014 in Denver in May): "Don't amplify the act of proceeding, amplify the value of it. Not 'Start free trial,' but 'End scheduling hassles.'"[3]

Earlier in this Writing Rule, I said to keep email copy short. But is shorter always better? Yes, except when it isn't. Probably my favorite email in my in-box comes weekly from a blog called *Brain Pickings* by Maria Popova, a self-described human-powered discovery engine for interestingness.

Unlike many emails in my in-box, it's not a quick read. It's impossibly long, with multiple links to *Brain Pickings* articles. Yet every week I set aside some time to pore through it, because when I read it I feel inspired, entertained, and a tiny bit smarter.

So what's the common thread between TaskRabbit and *Brain Pickings*, for all of us? It's to focus relentlessly on how you can help the people in your audience—by enriching their lives literally (TaskRabbit) or metaphorically (*Brain Pickings*).

Idea for a Nonresponsive Email List

If you've been in the email game for a while, you might find yourself with a list made up of people who routinely ignore your messages. Is all hope lost? Not necessarily. Try freshening up the relationship by doing something unexpected, suggests D. J. Waldow, coauthor of *The Rebel's Guide to Email Marketing*.

Segment your list to send a dedicated message to those who haven't opened an email recently, and make the content slightly offbeat—shocking, humorous, or whatever fits your brand best. "Whatever you normally do, do the opposite," Waldow told me. The idea is to incite reaction and (one would hope) reengagement.

It's tempting to hang on to those unresponsive addresses—it can be painful to think of purging names. But, as Waldow said, "Email messages work best when you speak to those who really want to hear from you." So if all your protracted attempts fail, do purge.

I can't talk about email without mentioning that the only true hard-and-fast rules that exist in the United States are those defined by the Controlling the Assault of Non-Solicited Pornography and Marketing Act of 2003, otherwise known as the CAN-SPAM Act. (And to be precise, this is a law, not a rule.) CAN-SPAM is the legislation passed by Congress to regulate commercial email.

In very simple terms, spam is email you didn't request—and don't want—from companies you might or might not know, selling products or services you might or might not want.

So if you are sending email to people on your list who didn't opt in to receiving them, and you don't respect the wishes of recipients who don't want to receive your email (i.e., those who opt out of receiving them), you're breaking the law, not just flouting a rule. So the best shortcut to avoiding problems—and, just as important, treating your email recipients with respect—is to make sure you have permission from recipients to email them.

(By the way, someone handing you a business card at an event does *not* constitute permission to add her to your email list.)

68

Writing Landing Pages
Less Is So Often More

One rainy afternoon when my son Evan was three or four, I took him to one of those cavernous beachside arcades. I thought the flashing lights, buzzing action, and acres of games (Frogger, Galaxian, Donkey Kong, and so on) would thrill him and we'd pass a happy few hours there.

Instead, he stood tentatively in the middle of the arcade, bewildered and overwhelmed. After halfheartedly tossing a few skee-balls up a ramp, he turned toward me and asked, "Is that enough, Mom? Can we go?"

Website landing pages often look and feel like an arcade floor. Rather than inviting visitors in and directing them through the site, landing pages confound visitors—who, of course, then act like my son did and bolt for the exit (by way of the back button).

A landing page is where visitors often end up after being enticed there by a specific, targeted campaign—an offer for something desirable delivered via email, social media, or an ad. And often the page places that compelling offer behind a lead capture form, with the idea of converting visitors into leads that can be followed up on. A landing page should offer visitors a hyperfocused experience that delivers them to a specific page and gives them a clear path to follow.

The graphic that follows is an example of one done badly. I stumbled on this when I clicked on a sponsored Facebook ad in my feed. (Side note: Sponsored Facebook ads offer a great pool of candidates for the Landing Page Hall of Shame. Click around on a few in your own feed. You'll see what I mean.)

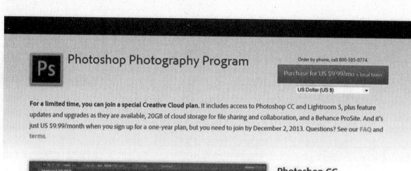

Photoshop CC

The industry standard for digital image processing and editing, Photoshop delivers a comprehensive package of professional retouching tools, and is packed with powerful editing features designed to inspire.

Lightroom 5

For editing digital photos without having to navigate the extensive offerings of Photoshop, Lightroom provides the precise tools photographers need to process their images efficiently, while still bringing out the best in their photographs.

I don't know what a "Creative Cloud" plan is. I don't understand the nuances of Photoshop and Lightroom. It makes sense when you dig around a bit, of course. But it makes me work it with a pretty sharp spade to get there.

Much better is this, also from Adobe:

Ah, that's better. It tells me what I can do with the Creative Cloud, and how I can access the necessary tools.

There is an art (and science) to creating a targeted landing page.

A highly effective one contains just enough information to inform visitors without making them feel as if fireworks are going off in their faces. Ideally, your landing page should convey three simple things: where your visitors are (where they've landed), what you're making available to them (and how awesome it is), and what the next step is to procure (or find out more about) that incredibly awesome thing.

It's tempting to go overboard—and arcade-ify your landing page by adding all manner of bells and whistles. Instead, go for simple and clean, with stupid-obvious navigation. As I've said elsewhere in this book: less is so often more.

Here is how you can put together the bones of an effective landing page—one that will convert your browsers into buyers (or subscribers), or at least further your relationship with them:

♦ **Match the message to the promise.** If your pitch promises something your prospect or customer wants (a buyer's guide to your product, a free e-book), make dead sure that the visitor receives precisely that—immediately.

"Message mismatch" is an all too common occurrence: in its study of 150 landing pages (see the feature at the end of this rule), Silverpop found that the most successful landing pages match the promotional copy in an email's call to action—that is, what yielded the click in the first place.

Yet 45 percent of the landing pages that were evaluated failed to repeat the email's promotional copy in the headline. If you sell someone on a promise, make sure that the first thing she experiences after taking action based on your promise doesn't tell a whole 'nother story.

♦ **Deliver awesome.** The other day I clicked on a link that offered a guide to family friendly Caribbean resorts, only to realize after I downloaded it that it was a sales brochure for one specific resort. I felt gamed, which is a bitter taste to leave in a prospect's mouth. Be sure that the content you produce as a landing-page download is valuable: Will your prospects love it? Or is it lame?

♦ **Avoid TMI.** Don't stuff too much information onto the page. (My boy in the arcade is the poster child for this one.) Doing so can invoke hyperlink distraction and result in your prospect wandering down a different path entirely. Scott Brinker, president and cofounder of marketing agency ion interactive, calls the tendency to weigh down a page with lengthy text and explanations "sagging page syndrome."

"Trying to cram as much as possible onto one page puts the burden on the respondent to sift through it," Brinker says. "Unfortunately, most of the time they're just not that into you yet."

♦ **Keep your headline benefit-driven.** Reiterate what's awesome about your offer by telling customers what's in it for them. A product-driven headline highlights what your product or service will do; a benefit-driven headline tells customers what your product or service will do for them.

In a test we did at MarketingProfs for two landing pages, both offering access to one of our planning tools, the first read, "Join today and get access to SmartTools: Social Media Marketing." The second read, "Create Successful Social Media Campaigns Fast with SmartTools."

The first is product-driven, but the second imparts what a subscriber will get out of it. Not surprisingly, the second, benefit-focused landing page converted 26 percent better than the product-focused page.

♦ **Subheads and copy. Be brief (mostly).** A subhead beneath the headline is a good place to explain the key benefits of your offering. *"Lots of words versus very few words"* is a richly debated issue in marketing circles. I'm a fan of fewer words, preferably in an easily scannable bullet form with perhaps a video or supporting graphics.

A word of caution: don't set video or audio to play automatically as soon as the page loads. Not only is that gratingly annoying, but the sudden volume can scare the bejesus out of us delicate types—or at least those who work in silence.

♦ **Use second person plus active verbs.** Someone who lands on a landing page is leaning forward—in other words, she has had her interest piqued. So speak to landing page visitors directly (lots of *you* and *your*) and use active verbs to match your tone to theirs. Something like *Get* or *Go* or *Start* or *Try* as opposed to the more generic *Submit*. (More on that below.)

♦ **Be blindingly obvious.** Once visitors land on the page and opt into your offer, make sure they know what to do next. Put a call to action in an obvious place, and play around with what language works best. Some research suggests that landing pages with submit buttons labeled simply *Submit* tend to perform worse than those that invoke more actionable wording, such as *Download now* or *Register* or *Get a quote*, as Progressive does here in its mobile landing page:

A landing page is a good place to use aspirational language, too, as Joanna Wiebe suggested in Rule 67 ("amplify the value, not action"), as in *Start saving* or *Simplify your banking* or *Get free advice . . .* (provided, of course, that you aren't being too cute and sacrificing clarity). Be sure the button stands out by adhering to the four Bs: big, bright, bold, and blindingly obvious.

♦ **Show, don't tell.** I like how email testing and analytics firm Litmus uses color and contrast to show you exactly what you're signing up for on its newsletter signup landing page. It's not quite as striking in black and white, but you get the idea:

Or how Progressive uses icons on its mobile landing page—the different options could've been listed in a dropdown text menu, but it's way better like this:

Multi Policy Discount! Get bigger savings when you insure more than just your car.

RV	Motorcycle	Boat
Home	Renters	Condo
Umbrella	Life	Health

- **Keep things simple.** For lead generation, solicit only the most relevant information via the form you ask your visitor to fill out. The idea is to eliminate friction and ease compliance: to entice, not irritate.

  "Simple" also means breaking up chunks of text, as well as pruning the words and images on the page down to the essentials. The less content you have on the page, the more you'll be able to feature "above the fold," the important space that page visitors see without having to scroll down.

- **Use trust indicators and social proof to reduce anxiety.** Establish credibility by including signals to your trustworthiness: testimonials, press mentions, third-party trust, and security verification (like TRUSTe or the Better Business Bureau), satisfaction guarantees, and so on.

  Some landing pages include "social proof," like blog comments or the number of followers on Facebook or Twitter. Social proof enhances credibility by signaling that others are similarly connected to your company, but I think such proof is better included on other content pages. Less is more, remember?

- **Test.** Your product and services are unique, and so is your audience. Test what works best for you—and with your audience. The most straightforward is a simple A/B test, in which you try two versions of an offer to see which performs better.

  Start by testing apples versus oranges, then refine your approach. Once you determine whether an apple converts better than an orange, determine whether a Red Delicious, say, converts better than a Granny Smith.

Unsuccessful Landings

In a study of the landing pages of 150 companies, Silverpop found that many failed to grab the attention of customers and prospects, thereby missing the opportunity to lead them down a clear path to conversion:

- Landing pages that failed to repeat the email's promotional copy in the headline: *45 percent.*

- Number of companies that confused customers with landing pages that didn't match the look and feel of the original offer: *3 out of 10.*
- Landing pages that included forms that required more than 10 fields to be completed: *45 percent.*
- Though the presence of a navigation bar on a landing page can be a distraction that pulls visitors away from the primary conversion goal, nearly *7 out of 10* landing pages included them.
- Professional writers know it's a lot harder to write short copy than long. Apparently, some marketers are taking the easy way out, since *25 percent* of the landing pages required scrolling through more than two screens of text.

Source: Loren McDonald, "Email Marketing Benchmarks: How Do You Stack Up Against the Best?", Silverpop webinar, May 22, 2014, www.silverpop.com/Documents/Whitepapers/2014/Email-Marketing-Metrics-Benchmark-Study-2014-Silverpop.pdf

69

Writing Headlines

*Learn How to Effortlessly Write an Intoxicatingly
Irresistible Headline—and You Won't Believe
What Happens Next!*

The other day I noticed a blog post on a marketing technology blog with a list of marketing industry public speakers that carried the headline "25 Jaw-Dropping Marketing Speakers."

You know what's jaw-dropping?

When Felix Baumgartner jumps live from the edge of space and lives to tell about it.

When your nephew kicks the winning goal into the end zone with seconds on the clock.

When your daughter struggles all year with Statistics and then works her tail off to stick an A.

When Santa delivers a brand-new bike on Christmas morning.

You know what's *not* jaw-dropping? A marketing speech. (Unless perhaps it's delivered naked on stage.)

Sites like BuzzFeed and Upworthy have become among the fastest-growing sites in the history of the Internet in part by mastering the writing of irresistible, weird, curiously grabby headlines that we are collectively too weak to resist—like the one heading up this section.[1] Or like "36 Of The Absolute Worst Things That Could Ever Happen to You" (BuzzFeed). Or "This Beautiful Ham Will Never Make It To Your Dinner Table. The Reason Why Is Just Plain Ridiculous" (Upworthy).

In some respects, I'm grateful for what the likes of BuzzFeed and Upworthy have done for headlines everywhere. They've helped under-score the idea that the best headlines are those that humans (and not just search engines) love, and they've helped propel us to a place where brands see the value of creating headlines (and content!) that people want to share with their friends.

The storyteller in me also appreciates that such headlines give a little more context and personality to a post. A headline from BuzzFeed such as "This Guy Is Painfully, Cringe-Inducingly Bad at Wheel of Fortune" paints a more vivid picture than a more straightforward headline ("Man Loses at Wheel of Fortune") might. And the use of *this* modifying *guy* inserts a specificity that subtly humanizes the story.

But at the same time it's troubling that marketers try to emulate the approach—for a few reasons.

First, most companies don't need their content to go BuzzFeed-viral, nor should they expect it to. Instead, content marketing goals are more modest in aggregate—but more lasting, too. Your goal is to help the people you are trying to reach and create value for them, to create content so useful they'll thank you for it, to build audience and relationships. With that in mind, then, a post Intuit ran on its blog in the fall of 2013—"What BuzzFeed Can Teach You About Writing a Viral-Worthy Headline"—seems kind of silly.[2]

Second, the BuzzFeed headline approach will ultimately erode your audience's trust in you, says David B. Thomas, senior director of content and engagement at Salesforce.com. "BuzzFeed has become one of the most popular sites in history, by taking a few content marketing principles and stretching them until they scream," David wrote on the Salesforce blog."[3]

And though it's tempting for marketers to copy the formula, David continues:

> *The problem is, people are getting sick of it. It might work, but apparently spam emails work, too. And robocalls. That doesn't mean we as marketers should emulate these tactics.*
>
> *Why are people getting sick of being promised "amazing" revelations and stories "they won"t believe"? Because usually those stories aren't amazing at all and are completely believable. At best, they're mildly interesting. When you write a grandiose headline like that, you're misleading your audience. You're promising something you can't deliver. You're setting them up and disappointing them. And since when has that been good business practice?*

The emphasis in David's last sentence is mine, because it's a point in need of emphasis!

What's the best approach for headlines, then? How do you write the kind of headlines that inspire connection and sharing, without duping or letting down your audience?

The key is this: spend as much time on the headline as you do on the writing itself. Respect the headline. The headline is not the metaphorical cherry on top, the dot over the *i*, the cross on the *t*, the icing on the cake, or the finishing flourish.

Today, especially, it's actually a key element of your post, article, or other piece of content. It tells the audience what you are going to deliver, and how you're going to deliver it, and why they should keep reading. So spend time with it, think on it, and figure out how to best use that valuable bit of text.

Keep in mind the following prescriptions when writing your headlines:

♦ **Create a curiosity gap, but with moderation.** Upworthy and BuzzFeed have built their businesses creating headlines with enough seduction in the headline to inspire a reader to click through to find out the rest of the story—Upworthy terms that a *curiosity gap*. (From Upworthy's blog: "a good social media headline seduces people to click through by telling them enough to whet their curiosity, but not enough to fulfill it.")[4]

The problem is that the technique gets a little tiresome, and (what's more) requires an increasing amount of hyperbole. If you're like me, you might feel a little ridiculous writing headlines like that. Because they are, after all, ridiculous.

But done right, the so-called curiosity-gap approach can inspire and inform and help readers by making it clear what a piece is about. The key is to keep yourself honest and use such headlines only when they are helpful triggers for your audience.

So go ahead and use "14 Surprising Ways You Can Grow Pumpkins," but only if the 14 ways might indeed be surprising to your audience. In the same vein, "14 Different Pumpkin Plants That Will Grow in Ridiculously Small Containers" will work only if the said containers actually are, well, ridiculously small.

♦ **Promise what you're going to deliver.** Your headline should promise the reader what you are going to deliver—as specifically as possible. What are readers going to get out of reading this piece? In what way will it inform them, or make their lives better?

♦ **Place your reader directly into the headline.** "14 Kinds of Pumpkins" is a boring title because it doesn't offer the reader anything specific. But "7 Kinds of Pumpkins You Can Grow on a City Balcony" speaks directly to him or her, offering a clear benefit. Even better might be something with a double benefit, such as "The 10-Minute Guide to Growing Giant Pumpkins on a City Balcony."

♦ **Be economical, and test.** Ideally, your headline should have fewer than 70 characters, as the chart in Rule 60 suggests. (Longer headlines will likely get truncated in search results and social shares.) You can, however, play with this a bit, if you are a fan of long headlines (as I am). Some content management systems (like WordPress) allow you to create one shortened headline for Google and another for the piece itself. You can also test headlines on social media channels to see which inspires the most shares and clicks.

♦ **Use numbers.** Numbers set expectations for readers. I like oddball numbers (like 3½, or 19, or 37). But see what works for you.

♦ **Use lively words.** Lively words paint a picture in the mind of your readers. Try including adjectives like *ultimate, brilliant, awesome, intense, hilarious, smart, critical, surprising*. As with the curiosity gap, though, the key is to not get too carried away. If something is surprising or awesome or ultimate . . . say so. If it's not, keep mum.

70

Writing a Home Page
We Get You

It's apt that we use the very human *home* to refer to the main page of a website, because that word evokes warmth and belonging.

That's exactly the mind-set to get into when you create content for your own business's home page—the Web page that is rendered when your business's domain name is typed into a Web-enabled device.

That page is a metaphorical threshold to your business.

Just as in your own actual home, you want visitors to feel welcomed as soon as they step in—to feel comfortable, to sense that you're happy to see them. And because this is your business, you want them to get a sense of their surroundings in the blink of an eye: an idea of who you are and what you do and—this is critical—why it matters to them.

What follows are some guidelines for writing home page content. But first, a caveat: There are many variables—related to the nature of your business and its goals—that determine what will make a successful home page for your business. So keep in mind that I'm advocating a general approach and not delivering a prescription.

+ **Speak to your audience.** Who is your audience? Whom do you want to attract? And—just as important—whom do you *not* want to attract? All good content is rooted in a clear understanding of your audience.

That sounds obvious, doesn't it? But it's surprising how often companies overlook their audiences and use their home pages to talk only about themselves.

For example, you might be tempted to use your home page to say you are "The world's leading business-to-business sales training and research firm." That might be true, but where is your audience in that description? Why should they care?

It's far better to say "You will make smarter sales decisions and grow your business faster with the help of our training and research." That tells people what's in it for them.

And, by the way, did you notice that I'm using *audience* and not *customers*? That's because your home page should also appeal to those who might not yet know who you are—and not just those with whom you have done business already.

It should be written and designed to appeal to those who might've stumbled to your doorstep—to impart to them a sense of why they belong there. (See my next point.)

♦ **They like me! They really like me!** Part of understanding your customers is truly knowing what motivates them. When you know what that is, you're able to communicate how you can help them.

You want your home page to say, "We get you. And, what's more, you belong here. We understand your challenges, your fears, your pain, your hopes, your needs. We shoulder your burdens. We've got your back. We'll give you a leg up."

Whichever of those metaphors you prefer, the main headline on your page should communicate that customer-centric value. Remember: your value is not what you do or what you sell, it's what you do *for your customers*. That shift may seem subtle, but it's everything.

The biggest wasted opportunity is to merely say, "Welcome." (Sorry, SUNY Albany.)

On the other hand, Ontario-based video marketing platform Vidyard (vidyard.com) communicates how it helps you. Video is hot, but a big problem for marketers is to prove that there'll be a return on investment. So right on its home page Vidyard makes its value clear with the customer-centric headline: "Turn viewers into customers." In doing so, it immediately tells its audience—you—not just what Vidyard does, but also how it helps you and your business.

♦ **Keep it stupid-simple.** Don't be tempted to fill space with lots of copy and graphics, especially above the fold—the part of a Web page that first appears in Web browsers when it's opened. This is what takes up the entire screen above the fold of the Dropbox (www.dropbox.com) home page:

There's more below that elaborates on "your stuff, any-where." But it's so simple, so calming, so Zen. And it feels like an antianxiety prescription—which, incidentally, is in a sense what Dropbox is all about.

Your own product or service might warrant a little more explanation, or it might be a little more complex. That's perfectly fine. Still, try to pare your statement of value to the essentials. Avoid the impulse to explain all you are and all that you do right away and up front, or you may overwhelm the visitor.

♦ **Use words your audience uses.** You don't need to embellish what you do. Use words that are familiar to your potential customer.

Did you notice that Dropbox uses *stuff* instead of *files, data, photos,* and so on? I suppose it could've come up with a more sophisticated sounding word (maybe assets? property? resources? content?). But *stuff* really does cover *all the things* we all have stored on our computers, phones, and tablets. And that's how many of us refer to all those things, right?

♦ **Use *you* promiscuously.** On your home page, use *you* more than you use *us* or *we.* As a kind of empathy hack or shortcut, an easy way to test your audience-centric approach is this: count how many times you use *you* on the home page, then count the number of times you use *us* or *we.* Make sure the *yous* are not just winning, but sweeping the series.

♦ **Now what?** Your headline communicates your clear value. Now, what do you want your visitors to do next?

Offer visitors three or four clear choices, or calls to action, each framed around a customer problem, with the mind-set of helping them and designed to draw a kind of path for them to follow. Consider both your content (the words you use) and the layout (including usability) when you design those calls to action.

I like the way business consulting firm SideraWorks ("collaborate better") neatly articulates a few familiar problems its audience can relate to in its effort to entice visitors further into the site.

For example, here's a path visitors might follow when the promise of collaborative software has fallen short (or when they merely want to know what might go wrong with its implementation) and they've come to SideraWorks (SideraWorks.com) to figure out the problem. The button shown in the graphic links to a post on the SideraWorks blog, which speaks to that pain point.

We Bought It, No One Is Using It

You could also try offering a party favor—freebies are great home page gifts to offer your audience, assuming what you offer is helpful and customer-centric. Consider a free download, free sample, free trial, free workbook, or free tool. Content marketing software and training company Copyblogger.com says this on its home page: "Grab 14 high-impact e-books and our 20-part Internet marketing course." (I like the action verb *grab* here.)

Even an email sign-up can be framed as a kind of gift that makes the value clear to the visitor—as opposed to what I often see, which is to take a corporate-centric approach, such as "Sign up for our email list."

(Pop quiz: Do any of us feel email-deprived? Answer: No.)

Takeout delivery service Eat24 offers clear value and conveys personality in its invitation to sign up for emails: "Want coupons, love notes, deep thoughts about bacon? Get our weekly email."

♦ **Convey trust.** Your home page should include elements that suggest others trust you. That can take many forms; you might show, for example, that you are a member of, or recognized by, a trusted community. That trust could be illustrated with social proof (links to Facebook, Instagram, YouTube, Twitter, and so on, with the number of followers or fans displayed)—in a quick reference ("Join 634,249 of your peers . . .") or addressed more fully. For example, hotel alternative Airbnb addresses trust and safety right on its home page, with a link to a fuller explanation of how it verifies and stands behind its properties.

71

Writing the About Us Page
When It's Not Really About You

The key to a successful About Us page sounds paradoxical: the best About Us pages aren't really about the company; instead, they focus on relaying who they are *in relation to the visitor.*

All good content puts the reader first, and that's no different on your About Us page. In other words, About Us gives you a chance to talk about yourself, but always in the context of what you do for your customers. What burdens you help them shoulder, what problems you solve for them.

This page can be a handy place to show some personality, to differentiate yourself, to tell a story. Yet many About Us pages seem ignored. Here's an example of a buttoned-up, anonymous About Us page from Toys "R" Us. I'd file this under SO, for squandered opportunity:

Contrast that with how Coca-Cola tells its company story:

Yes, Coca-Cola's page is bold and graphical and nicely designed. But it's also an inspired look at the company's rich history, presented in a way that's interesting to the reader, and the page is fundamentally useful. This is pretty much the poster child for an About Us page that follows my content formula in the Introduction: Useful × Inspired × Empathic.

One of my favorite About Us approaches is the video narrative tack taken by Chicago law firm Levenfeld Pearlstein (lplegal.com), because of the way it uses the opportunity to differentiate itself as a very human and approachable law firm (I talked about this in more detail in Rule 41).

Here are some other rules to follow when creating your About Us page:

- **Show a human, accessible side.** Write with a clear voice and a conversational tone that matches the rest of your site and your other properties. You might be tempted to include superlatives like *best in class* or *world-renowned* or *cutting-edge*.

    We talked about this in general earlier in the book with respect to your content and writing. But I'm giving you a reminder here in the same way that friends sometimes give a recovering alcoholic a reminder to keep on walking past his favorite bar. Temptation can be strong. But so are you.

- **Show your people as real people.** Levenfeld Pearlstein shows the human side of its lawyers very well via video narrative, but you have many other options—photos, links to social profiles, favorite quotes, what your staff members do in their spare time, what they eat for breakfast, what music they listen to, their favorite place to travel, and so on.

- **Include an Easter Egg.** Surprise visitors to your About Us page with something unexpected. Video hosting company Wistia gets creative with its About Us/Company page.

    The Wistia "yearbook" looks pretty straightforward:

Source: Reproduced with courtesy of Wistia, Inc.

But when you mouse over each one of those photos, it's swapped out for a series of other stills that makes each employee appear to dance in the frame; Marketing's Ezra Fishman executes a flawless chicken dance. It's hard to recreate it in stills on a page, but you get the idea:

Source: Reproduced with courtesy of Wistia, Inc.

♦ **Bring your customers into your story.** Why do your customers care about what you do? How have you helped them? Customer testimonials are great here. They're even better if they pulse with life: can you get them on video? Or can you create a video that highlights what people say about you?

72

Writing Infographics That Won't Make People Mock Infographics

Pity the humble infographic. Why? Because, like a Kardashian, it's ubiquitous and it inspires strong, often negative reactions.

SaveDelete, a blog that publishes tech and computer marketing tips and news, once ran a roundup of the "Top 13 Infographics that Mock Infographics." (Among them, the very meta data set "The Number of 'Infographics' I've Seen This Week," and "Infographs Are Ruining the Internet.")[1]

But when done right, infographics can be a powerful marketing tool. They're easily shareable and portable, functioning as content party favors that allow your audience to repost the material on their own blogs or sites, thereby spreading your message for you.

An *infographic* is what it sounds like—information expressed graphically via drawings, pictures, maps, diagrams, charts, or similar elements—all held together with a coherent visual theme and typically published as an image file. They are also produced in video form.

Infographics are not about self-promotion. The best of them express rich, objective data in a way that's more accessible and engaging than a dense spreadsheet or ho-hum pie chart. Generally they take one of four shapes, says Joe Chernov of HubSpot: an illustration of the "state of" some business sector or function; a checklist or resource; a compare-and-contrast study; and the evolution of a movement, demographic, or industry.

Popularized in the 1930s and '40s for editorial use in magazines (though they've been around much longer), infographics have found broader applications in business for research findings as well as for content marketing, write Jason Lankow, Josh Ritchie, and Ross Crooks in their book *Infographics: The Power of Visual Storytelling* (Wiley 2012).

When they're done right, they communicate with artful impact. Josh Ritchie, cofounder and creative director of Column Five, an infographic and data-design company based in San Francisco, says a favorite infographic of his is one created by Charles Joseph Minard in 1869. A pioneer in using graphics in engineering and statistics, Minard produced *Carte figurative des pertes successives en hommes de l'Armée Française dans la campagne de Russie 1812–1813*, a flow map depicting Napoleon's disastrous Russian campaign of 1812. Later, scientist and inventor Étienne-Jules Marey said Minard's infographic "defies the pen of the historian in its brutal eloquence."

Joe Chernov notes simply: "Quality infographics are inherently informative and visually engaging. They're expertise in a blink."

Let's break down infographics into their constituent parts:

♦ **Utility.** The best infographics are entertaining, educational, and intrinsically useful. Ask yourself: How will this help my audience? Will they find this applicable to their business? Will they be fascinated enough to spend a few minutes with it, then pass it around?

♦ **Data.** Infographics should be based on fact, not merely opinion. So use credible data (as you should for all content, but it's especially true here). Your ideas might emerge as part of that story, but credible infographics are rooted first in reality. Remember: *if you are going to tell me what you think, give me a solid foundation for your reasoning.* Your infographic should tease a larger story out of facts, not feelings.

What's a credible source? A research report from a reputable analyst or industry association is a good source; a blog post, less so. (See Rule 59.)

♦ **Story.** The best infographics have a hypothesis and narrative at their core. That sounds high-minded, doesn't it? But it just means that you need to home in on the key idea you want your data to express. Write a kind of thesis statement. Then outline the main data points you want to use that support your thesis.

"Don't forget to put the *info* in *infographic*," says Veronica Jarski, a visual artist and content creator for MarketingProfs. "If you have a lovely graphic but boring or poorly written information . . . well, then, you only have a lovely graphic."

And by the way, when dealing with data, less is more: don't try to cram too much into an infographic. Distill the essence of your message; if you still have more to say on the subject, link to a full report that has more information.

Cisco did that with its video on cloud computing, "Consider the Cupcake," which used a baking analogy to forecast the enormity of cloud computing in 2015. Cisco had a lot to say on the topic, so it linked to a landing page that allowed visitors who wanted more to download an entire research report on the subject.[2]

♦ **Logical sequence.** Lay out the narrative with an eye toward information architecture. This means organizing your information in a way that flows logically, without undue complexity. Create an outline that highlights your key ideas in a narrative form. You might be tempted to skip this phase and go straight to design. But mapping is the critical step to creating an infographic that tells a meaningful story and doesn't read as a jumble of numbers and drawings.

"When you go to an art gallery, you notice little plaques next to the artwork that share crucial information to the artwork itself," said Jarski. "Now imagine, you're looking at Van Gogh's *Starry Night* and the plaque beside offers details about the *Mona Lisa*. Jarring, right? The images and text need to make sense together."

♦ **Great design.** Awesome infographics use color, typography, illustrations, animation, video, charts, and text to convey their data story. Hiring an agency like Column Five is one option. But there are resources for DIYers as well. (See The DIY Infographic Tool Belt feature at the end of this section.)

Need some inspiration? Go to Pinterest.com and search for *infographics*. I'll warn you now: be prepared to kill an hour or two. The overabundance makes Thanksgiving dinner seem like a snack.

♦ **Quality control.** Make sure your infographic is error-free. Check and double-check figures, source lines, and text. Unlike other forms of content, it's hard to re-call an infographic once it's out in the world. We get a surprising number of infographics in the MarketingProfs in-box containing typos or math errors. To paraphrase Norm Abram's *measure twice, cut once* mantra: check twice, create once. If your infographic gets toted over to blogs and embedded (as you hope it will), you want it to look professional.

♦ **Promotion.** The goal, as ever, is to drive attention to and interest in your brand. So be sure to cover the basics. The best infographics are outfitted with social bling to allow visitors to easily share them on LinkedIn, Pinterest, Twitter, and Facebook, including a string of code that allows them to be embedded on other sites, with a link back to you.

Joe Chernov suggests including a call to action in the infographic as well—but nothing too complicated. "I recommend more of a stay-in-touch approach—like 'sign up for future updates' or 'get the full report here,'" he says, versus something time- or sales-specific, like a free trial offer. That's because an infographic can have a long shelf life, and you want yours to make the most of it.

The DIY Infographic Tool Belt

Google Public Data Explorer

The Google Public Data Explorer tool allows you to choose from numerous (neatly organized) public data sets pulled from the U.S. Census Bureau. Or roll your own infographics by uploading your own data (www.google.com/publicdata/directory).

Many Eyes

Created by IBM Research, the Many Eyes tool helps you build infographics based on your data, or on public data sets that include everything from U.S. population density to Internet browsers by popularity (www-958.ibm.com/software/data/cognos/manyeyes).

Piktochart

Piktochart offers a free DIY infographics tool with lots of fun, flexible templates. Even more templates come with the modestly priced paid version (http://app.piktochart.com).

Hohli

Hohli is an online chart builder that allows you to create Venn diagrams, bar graphs, scatter plots, and other charts—with the flexibility to customize their look and feel (http://charts.hohli.com).

Wordle

Wordle allows you to generate a word cloud from any block of text. Part tool and part toy, Wordle is a fun and colorful way to create a picture of how the brand looks (literally) based on the language it uses (http://wordle.net).

Visual.ly

Visual.ly is a showcase for data visualization and a great resource for those looking to create or share infographics (as well as a kind of Match.com for brands and infographic designers). But the Create part of the site offers a DIY tool (http://create.visual.ly).

infogr.am

infogr.am allows users to create infographics easily and fairly quickly based on one of several predesigned templates that allow for various kinds of customization (http://infogr.am).

Visage

Visage is a visual content platform created by Column Five. It's not free, but it's competitively priced. It's positioned as an option for brands looking for a step up from available free tools but unable to justify paying a design agency for ongoing design work (http://visage.com).

Source: Joe Chernov and MarketingProfs.com.

73

Writing Better Blog Posts

A few weeks ago, I asked author and entrepreneur Guy Kawasaki whether writing matters in blog posts. By this point in the book you and I are friends, so you know my position.

I admit I was goading Guy a little. But my heart grew two sizes when Guy said, "This is like asking if the quality of food in a restaurant matters. Writing is the primary determinant of the success of the post. Everything else—timing, graphics, frequency—is secondary."

The best advice I can offer about writing better blog posts, then, is to simply follow the prescription for better writing in the previous sections of this book. (What will your audience thank you for?) There's nothing more magical I can offer than that.

But here are some tactical suggestions that have more to do with structuring a post than with the writing itself:

- **Keep headlines tight.** Guy suggests headlines of four or five words. Play with length, though: length matters less than specificity and your own audience's preferences.

  Most blog post titles are around 40 characters in length. However, those with titles a bit longer than average—around 60 characters—received the most social shares, according to a recent study by TrackMaven. (Blog posts with titles of more than 60 characters had sharp declines in social shares.)
- **Add blog bling.** Every post should have a large graphic or embedded video. Make it count: "No stock photos of an Asian, an African American, and a woman staring at a laptop," Guy says. (See Part VI for photo resources.)

- **Time it well.** Usually the best time for publication is between 8 and 10 a.m. weekdays, in the time zone where your readers live, Guy says.

  TrackMaven's research suggests that Tuesday and Wednesday are the most popular days for posting. However, the 13 percent of pieces published on weekends actually had more social shares per post on average, and Saturdays were particularly ripe for blog post sharing: only 6.3 percent of posts were published on Saturdays, but they received 18 percent of the total social shares.[1]

- **Use bullets and numbered lists.** "Bullets and numbers indicate an organized mind and empathy for the time constraints of readers," Guy said. I couldn't agree more. Also, they tend to create white space.

- **Provide sharing and subscriber options.** Don't leave your visitors hanging! Give them a path to conversion—however you are defining the conversion action (download, sale, signup, and so on).

- **Keep them short. Ish.** Posts should have fewer than 1,500 words (per Andy Crestodina's chart in Rule 60) and they should be structured with subheads and bolding.

  Guy likes fewer than 1,000 words. "I cannot remember reading any blog post that I wished was longer," Guy said. "I can remember reading many, many blog posts that were too long—tellingly, I cannot remember what they were about!"

- **Use an interesting approach.** Remember the mandate in Rule 8: good writing has logic and structure. But the structure itself can help to draw your readers in; revisit Rule 8 for some ideas about approaches and organizing.

- **Show up.** Half of blogging is consistency, or just showing up on a regular basis. As writer and content marketer Barry Feldman told me: "Write. Write now. Write a lot. Write freely. Write what you feel. Write first and edit second. If you want hits, you need to keep going up to the plate and swinging."

- **Build scale.** To establish yourself, write for your audience's audience. A great way to build scale for your blog is to ensure that your writing appeals to industry influencers, says Buffer CEO Leo Widrich.

Buffer, a social media tool, used to focus its content on sharing ways to use Twitter and then (later) other social platforms more effectively. But then Leo had an epiphany, he said. In the second half of 2012 and throughout 2013 Buffer expanded its blogging strategy, focusing on lifehacking, business, customer service, and other topics alongside social media, because he realized it was key to getting access to a larger audience, he said.

"This helped us tremendously in terms of branding and getting a much wider audience," Leo said in an email interview. "We hit 1 million page views per month and managed to get ourselves republished on Time.com, Fast Company, The Next Web and many other outlets with this broader content approach."

In 2014, Buffer split its blogging efforts into two blogs, refocusing on social media tips in its main blog (blog.bufferapp.com) and launching a second blog it calls Open (open.bufferapp.com) as an expanded, more general outlet to talk about company culture and lifehacking tips.

"Reaching our audience's audience is a big goal for us," Leo said, a strategy he said was inspired by Rand Fishkin's content marketing manifesto at Moz.com.

"The reason for doing this is that ultimately it's the best way how your brand and your audience can grow. You don't limit yourself to just a certain audience, but you make sure that your content is relevant to your audience's audience at all times."

♦ **Experiment.** Innovate. Do something unexpected. I can try to convey best practices and broad benchmarks. But you know what really works? It's this: figuring out what works for your audience, doing that, and doing it again and again, consistently.

Consider the tremendous opportunity you have before you as just that—a tremendous opportunity. So experiment. Optimize. And have fun.

74

Writing Annual Reports (or Annual Wrap-Ups)

Even if you aren't required to put together an annual report for investors or donors, you might consider writing some sort of annual wrap-up.

Why? Because annual reports provide you with an opportunity to tell your brand's story, giving your audience a way to connect with you and travel along with you as you mark your milestones.

Creating a dry-as-dust document filled with nothing more than plain text and financial data is a waste of a one-of-a-kind opportunity to showcase your company. Nobody wants to read that sort of annual report (except for possibly an insomniac trying to catch some extra sleep). But everybody loves a great story, right?

Your report should feature real people, real situations, genuine emotions, and facts.

It should show, not tell, as much as possible. It should explain—in terms people can relate to—how your company adds value to the lives of your customers. Recall Donald Murray's words here: "The reader doesn't turn the page because of a hunger to applaud." Write something that encourages them to keep following you, and get a little more involved in your story.

Start with some basics:

- Who did we grow to become in the past year? What changed? What didn't?
- How have we evolved since our founding?

♦ What have been our biggest successes and our crushing failures?

♦ What's commonplace to us that might be interesting to others?

So who has done annual reports or wrap-ups well? Here are two companies (one business-to-business and one business-to-consumer) that recently told their true, human, customer-centric stories in an original way.

1. *HubSpot's 2013 Year-in-Review.* The Boston-based technology company produced a magazine-like look back at some of its key achievements of the previous year.

   • *What it is.* Produced with a tool called Uberflip, HubSpot's *2013 Year-in-Review* reads more like an issue of *People* magazine than a business-to-business company production.[1] Magazine sections include financial information, charitable efforts, events, and so on.

   Data is presented in an accessible, eye-catching way—more infographic than spreadsheet. There are candids of new hires, and staff stars get the same treatment that celebrities get in *People* in a lighthearted section titled They're Just Like Us! ("They play with their dogs!" "They take selfies!")

   • *Why it works.* HubSpot could've produced a static e-book or PPT deck with the same information. But by looking to analogy instead of example—borrowing a page (so to speak) from consumer magazines—HubSpot's fresh approach breaks new ground. *They looked to analogy, rather than example.*

   • *Idea you can steal.* What's new in your industry is new. Look to other parts of your life for inspiration for an approach that would be unique to your market, even if not necessarily brand-new, period.

2. *Warby Parker's annual report.* The eyewear retailer annually reimagines the generally boring annual report and comes up with something entirely new—and in doing so tells a bigger story about Warby culture.[2]

   • *What it is.* The 2013 report, released in January 2014, is the third such year-end effort. This one is a kind of online calendar that looks back on each day of the year that was and recognizes something significant that happened during that 24-hour period.

Warby, which is privately held, calls out not only successes (the debut of its first commercial) but also slip-ups (shipping errors), as well as a bunch of quirky facts (that time 60 employees took a spinning class together). Together the review tells a bigger story of Warby's culture, people, customers, and values. It was produced in-house by Warby's own content and design teams.

- *Why it works.* Annual reports and their ilk generally underscore only the best bits of a business—the parts that show them in the best light—and hide the bad stuff in four-point print. Warby instead chose a different approach: highlighting in an original, accessible way its more human, sometimes vulnerable, yet wholly relatable side.

  And by the way, if Warby's effort seems overly ambitious for a year-end wrap-up: it also works to ignite sales. Following the release of its annual report in the previous two years, Warby experienced record sale days, according to a report published in *Ad Age*.[3]

  How many annual reports actually drive sales, aside from Warby's? I'd guess zero percent.

- *Idea you can steal.* What are you already doing that you could reimagine, using more originality to more broadly reflect your unique story?

Three more quick examples:

1. *MailChimp's By-the-Numbers.* The email marketing company creates a visually dynamic annual report/microsite called By the Numbers.[4]

   As viewers scroll down the one-page site, MailChimp offers a literal journey of stats and figures and fun facts about both the company's and its individual team members' 2013 accomplishments. Things like Zero MailChimp team softball wins, 8 new MailChimp babies, 228,627 A/B tests run, and 70,000,000,000 emails sent.

The report concludes with a thank-you note for another great year. Even though MailChimp delivers simple stats, it takes the opportunity to humanize the company a bit, too.

2. *Calgary Zoo's Instagram day-in-the-life annual report.* I loved the creative twist on an annual report designed by the Calgary Zoo.[5] In 2012 the zoo created an Instagram account (@calgaryzoo2012ar) and added a series of 55 photos over a one-week period. Taken in aggregate, the captions of the photos deliver facts and figures about the zoo's initiatives, and the photos themselves provide an intimate walk-through-the-zoo theme for the almost completely visual report. Among the final posts is a message from the president of the zoo:

Source: Reproduced with courtesy of Calgary Zoo.

3. *MarketingProfs infographic.* At MarketingProfs, we told a visual story of where we stood at the end of the year, because it was the most straightforward way to underscore our varied expertise, audiences, and revenue streams. The infographic does double-duty on our About Us page:

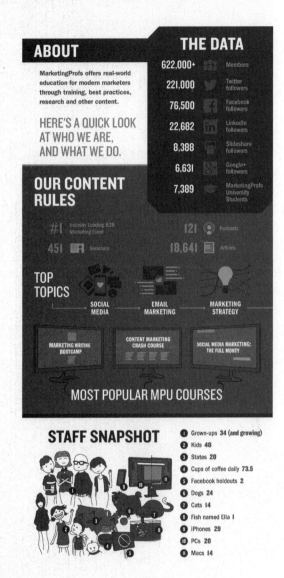

Buffer did this, too—not as a year-end review, but when it acquired its one millionth customer.[6]

Part VI

Content Tools

What content tools will help you produce your best work?

John Steinbeck reportedly used 300 Eberhard Faber Blackwing 602 pencils to complete *East of Eden* and another 60 to produce *The Grapes of Wrath*. The Blackwing's performance (expressed in its famous slogan, "Half the pressure, twice the speed") gave the pencil a cult following that continued even after it was discontinued in 1998—because who wouldn't want to use the same tool that Steinbeck and Vladimir Nabokov and Joseph Finder and Stephen Sondheim used?

Other writers have been equally persnickety about their writing tools. In his Paris memoir, *A Moveable Feast*, Hemingway details his requirements: "The blue-backed notebooks, the two pencils and the pencil sharpener (a pocket knife was too wasteful), the marble-topped tables, the smell of *café crèmes*, the smell of early morning sweeping out and mopping and luck were all you needed."

Neil Gaiman and Stephen King reportedly use fountain pens, because they both like to write more slowly and with more intention.

"I discovered I loved the fact that handwriting forces you to do a second draft, rather than just tidying up and deleting bits on a computer," Neil told the BBC.[1] "I also discovered I enjoy the tactile buzz of the ritual involved in filling the pens with ink." (I like that he says he changes the ink color each day so he can discern how many pages he produced the previous day.)

Jane Austen wrote on sheepskin with a quill pen, using a special kind of ink made with stale beer. The *Palimpsest* blog has her recipe:[2]

Take 4 ozs of blue gauls [gallic acid, made from oak apples], 2 ozs of green copperas [iron sulphate], 1 1/2 ozs of gum arabic. Break the gauls. The gum and copperas must be beaten in a mortar and put into a pint of strong stale beer; with a pint of small beer. Put in a little refin'd sugar. It must stand in the chimney corner fourteen days and be shaken two or three times a day.

I suppose there's nothing magical about Blackwing pencils and fountain pens and beer-based ink. Unless, of course, maybe there is.

Throughout this book, I've listed tools related to specific content tasks. For example, tools that help design or create infographics are listed in the infographics section, and Rule 25 includes some tools that evaluate readability.

What follows in this section are some other content creation tools you might find useful for actual writing, as well as tools that help organize and plan your writing or content projects. In some cases I've added commentary when I thought something needed a bit more explanation or clarification.

These are not the tools and processes of recognized literary geniuses, but those of ordinary people like you and me—based on the recommendations of friends, marketers, book authors, and businesspeople I polled with one question: *What's a content tool you can't live without?*

Because, you know, in our modern marketing world, all of us are a wee bit persnickety.

Because *everybody writes*!

Research and Knowledge Management Tools

These tools allow you to save research and capture and organize notes (which might be photos, audio notes, handwritten notes, screenshots, Web pages, and so on) and sync them between devices. There are some nuances relating to the performance and capabilities of each. But generally speaking these tools provide you with a more workable approach to research than, say, Post-it notes and highlighters or scraps of paper and filing cabinets.

Knowledge management sounds a little high-minded, maybe. But I couldn't think of a better term with the same precision. *Brain organizer? Concept planner?* Eww. Knowledge management it is.

- ♦ *Evernote* (evernote.com) gets top billing because almost everyone seems to love it. I've never gotten the hang of Evernote, but clearly I'm missing something. My friend Andrew Davis (author of *Brandscaping*) says I need to keep trying. My mother told me the same thing about Swiss chard when I was eight. I now eat Swiss chard. So maybe Andrew is right.

♦ *Diigo* (diigo.com).
♦ *Microsoft OneNote* (onenote.com).
♦ *Springpad* (springpad.com).
♦ *SimpleNote* (simplenote.com).
♦ *Workflowy* (workflowy.com).
♦ *Pocket* (getpocket.com).
♦ *Wridea* (wridea.com).
♦ *Google Keep* (keep.google.com) is more like iOS Notes for Android, and less robust than others here.

Writing Tools

What's interesting is that many of the tools modern writers say they prefer aren't very modern at all. Like Nabokov and Steinbeck and Gaiman, many of us rely on pedestrian things such as notebooks, sketchpads, pens, and pencils—especially for The Ugly First Draft. And many of us use things like Post-it notes, whiteboards, and rolls of butcher paper to help modularize gargantuan writing tasks.

Why is that? I think my friend Jesse Noyes from Kapost is onto something when he suggests that using off-line tools eliminates friction between the writer and the writing.

Nonetheless, here are some popular online writing tools.

♦ *Scrivener* (literatureandlatte.com) is writing software that is especially great for composing, structuring, and manipulating long and difficult documents—like books, e-books, manuals, or lengthy white papers. (I'm using it right now.) It's overkill for smaller writing tasks, though—say, blog posts or articles.
♦ *yWriter* (spacejock.com/yWriter5.html) is similar to Scrivener, but is only for PCs.
♦ *Ulysses* (ulyssesapp.com).
♦ *Mellel* (mellel.com).
♦ *Microsoft Word* (office.com) I feel a little silly listing Word here—it's a little like listing *water* or *bread basket* on a restaurant menu, because it's that ubiquitous. But I'm including it here so that I don't get letters.
♦ *Pages* (apple.com/mac/pages).

♦ *Text editors*, of which there are many—TextEdit (iOS), MS Notepad, and Byword are a few. All are stripped-down, simple platforms preferred because of their Zen qualities and because they don't throw lots of extra code and characters into text the way (for example) MS Word does when you import a document into a content management system like WordPress. Michael Brenner of NewsCred writes his blog posts as draft emails and pops them into WordPress, effectively hacking a text editor by using something that's more familiar to most of us.

♦ *Draft* (draftin.com) was started by engineer Nathan Kontny to help people become better writers. I like the on-demand copy-editing feature (which is kind of like an Uber for editing). I also like the Hemingway mode (based on the line "Write drunk, edit sober" often attributed to him), which doesn't allow you to delete anything you've written.

Productivity Tools

What's it take to get up off the couch or quit screwing around on Facebook and actually do the work? Writing seems to trigger a latent ADHD condition in almost everyone, and procrastination and distraction become permanent handicaps. Which is why this section reads a little like the self-help shelves at your Barnes & Noble.

The goal of all of these productivity tools is to make you a more efficient, productive, and less suicidal writer.

♦ *WeaveWriter* (weavewriter.com) is a three-part, self-guided course to help you develop better lifelong writing habits. It was developed by my friend Dane Saunders after he burned himself out by writing two books in a year (and then promptly collapsed).

♦ *Scapple* (literatureandlatte.com/scapple.php) is from the folks at Scrivener. It's designed to help you brainstorm by mapping and tracking ideas and identifying connections between them. It's not exactly a mind-mapping tool for writers, but it's close.

♦ *Write or Die* (writeordie.com) is a writing app that bills itself as putting the *prod* in productivity. It allows you to set a time limit and attaches random consequences if you quit typing (sirens, pop-up boxes, heart attack-inducing unwriting). It's either motivating or anxiety-producing, depending on your temperament. If you are a nervous person who cries easily, try another platform.

♦ *Written?Kitten!* (writtenkitten.net) is like Write or Die but "cuter and fuzzier," it says, because it delivers a fresh kitten for a predetermined number of words.

♦ *750Words* (750words.com) is a site that delivers points and badges based on output. It's based on the idea from *The Artist's Way* of writing three pages (or 750 words) daily as a kind of religion.

♦ *Ommwriter* (ommwriter.com) is a writing app that offers a clean, minimalist writing experience for focused, distraction-free writing.

♦ *Zen Writer* (beenokle.com/zenwriter.html) is another app, similar to Ommwriter.

♦ *WriteRoom* (hogbaysoftware.com/products/writeroom) delivers another distraction-free writing environment, for Mac.

♦ *Quabel* (quabel.com) is another uncluttered writing app.

♦ *Cold Turkey* (getcoldturkey.com) allows you to blacklist or block certain sites or mail servers for a set period of time if you are powerless against the compulsion to check email and Facebook and whatever else when you should be writing (for Windows).

♦ *SelfControl* (selfcontrolapp.com) is an app similar to Cold Turkey, but for Mac.

♦ *Offtime* (offtime.co) is similar to Cold Turkey and SelfControl; it is currently invite-only.

♦ *StayFocusd* (chrome.google.com) is a Chrome extension that allows you to limit the time you spend on whatever websites you consider irresistible time-sinks.

♦ *LeechBlock* (https://addons.mozilla.org) is the same as StayFocusd, but for Firefox.

♦ *Pomodoro Technique* (pomodorotechnique.com) is more of a time management and productivity technique than an actual app or tool—unless you count the cute 25-minute, tomato-shaped timer as a tool. But I suppose it is. My friend Sonia Simone (Copyblogger) riffs on this idea by focusing in 20-minute increments. Not sure which fruit—if any—she uses as a timer.

♦ *Tomatoes* (tomato.es) is an online timer, without an actual tomato. You can set Tomatoes to actually hear the minutes ticking by. Motivating or maddening? Your call.

- *Unstuck* (unstuck.com) describes itself as a digital coach that helps us get unstuck by offering us fresh perspective via a series of provocative questions, targeted tips, and action-oriented tools. It's handy if you're feeling paralyzed by a project. On the other hand, it's ironically also a handy place to go to avoid that project even more.

Editing Tools

The editing tools that follow can help with word choice or with the readability of your prose. I've included those listed under Rule 25 in Part I just to bring together these resources all in one place.

Keep in mind that none of these tools should be substitutes for human editors—or your own sensibility as a writer, for that matter. But they can provide excellent first passes before your text lands on the desk of an editor or copyeditor.

- *Grammarly* (grammarly.com) bills itself as an automated proofreader and "your personal grammar coach." It's both a Web app and a plug-in for Word and Outlook, and so it is fairly robust. A machine is doing the work, of course, but using Grammarly almost feels as if you have a gentle but dogged copyeditor on your side who is determined to improve your text's readability.
- *Hemingway* (hemingwayapp.com) is an app that flags flaccid sentences and weak writing in favor of writing that's sharp and concise. I really love this app—it's fun to play with, and it can highlight troubling spots in your writing. But keep in mind that when I ran part of Hemingway's own *Farewell to Arms* through the tool, it flagged instances of overly complex prose, passive voice, and too many adverbs. Just sayin'.
- *ProWritingAid* (prowritingaid.com) is an online writing coach that flags spelling and grammar errors, clichés, and redundancies; it also checks for plagiarism and readability.
- *Autocrit* (autocrit.com) is similar to ProWritingAid.
- *SmartEdit* (smart-edit.com) is similar to the two previous tools.
- *Wordcounter* (wordcounter.com) checks for redundancies in your text by ranking the most frequently used words (helpful if everything is a *solution* or *service*).

- *Cliché Finder* (cliche.theinfo.org) simply does what the name says: it finds clichés.
- *Plagium* (plagium.com) lets you check where your text appears on the Web.
- *Visual Thesaurus* (visualthesaurus.com) is one of many word finders on the Web, but I like Visual Thesaurus because it's a mash-up of a thesaurus and a dictionary, and because it creates word maps that are both elegant and useful.
- *Word Hippo* (wordhippo.com) is like a lot of sites that relate to writing in that it has an old-school look and feel that makes it seem it hasn't been updated since Amazon sold only books. But it's an incredible, useful site because it allows you to search word categories (such as "rhyme with") in addition to antonyms, translations, or even a 10-letter word that starts with a *B*. (Why might you need that, specifically? I don't know right now. But you never know.)
- *Inbound Writer* (inboundwriter.com) is like a writing coach (available on the Web or as a WordPress plug-in) that allows you to score and tweak your content based on SEO (search engine optimization) and social media research terms.
- *Read-able* (read-able.com) is a readability scoring app that's an alternative to the Flesch-Kincaid score feature that's built into Microsoft Word.
- *Edit Central* (editcentral.com/gwt1/EditCentral.html#style_diction) is a readability scoring tool that's limited to 50,000 characters at a time.
- *Readability Formulas* (readabilityformulas.com/free-readability-formula-tests.php) is an app that's limited to 600 words at a time, but it runs your content through seven formulas.
- *Online-Utility.org* (online-utility.org/english/readability_test_and_improve.jsp) is a tool that indentifies sentences that may need revision.

A Few Great Style Guides

Style guides are writing and editing guides that most newspapers, magazines, and websites follow to maintain accuracy, clarity, and consistency in their content. Is it email or e-mail or E-mail? Do we spell out *seven* or use the numeral 7? These maybe feel like small issues. But inconsistent copyediting makes you look like a rookie.

Some companies don't have their own style guides (i.e., a *house guide*); instead, they follow well-known style guides such as the *Associated Press Stylebook*, the *Chicago Manual of Style*, or the *Yahoo! Style Guide* (more on the latter below). Also, certain industries have their own stalwarts—like the *AMA Manual of Style* (www .amamanualofstyle.com), the recognized leader in medical and scientific publishing.

The best reason for producing your own style guide to either augment or supplant existing style guides is that it will reflect your company's own requirements and preferences. For example, you might want to refer to commonly used industry terms a specific way, or you might prefer to treat your products or lines of business or executives a certain way editorially. It can also be helpful if you work with a lot of freelance content creators, because it puts everyone on the same page. Literally.

Here are some useful style guides to refer to:

♦ *The Economist Style Guide* (economist.com/styleguide) is one I fell in love with at its first line: "The first requirement of *The Economist* is that it should be readily understandable." And that was only the start of our relationship. It goes on to offer great, practical, real-world advice for content of any type. Word nerds will appreciate its commentary and updates via Twitter, too (twitter.com/econstyleguide).

♦ *BuzzFeed Style Guide* (buzzfeed.com/emmyf/buzzfeed-style-guide) is a style guide that elevates style guides from the back room to the front page. It's funny and irreverent (where else would you learn the preferred spelling for *batshit* or *bitchface*?), but it's also useful. I learned a few things from the section on LGBT.

♦ *The Guardian Style Guide* (www.theguardian.com/guardian-observer-style-guide-a) is a solid style guide; it's also on Twitter (twitter.com/guardianstyle).

♦ *The Yahoo! Style Guide* (St. Martin's Griffin Press, 2010) is a great general online publishing resource. The book covers pesky details too pesky to get into here, and answers elementary questions such as where to put a period. Quibble: It was published in 2010, so it deserves a good dusting and freshening up.

Non-Text Writing Tools

I was surprised at the number of people who told me that they use tools, such as the ones that follow, to record first drafts of blog posts while driving, and then shape them into a readable format later. Who knew?

♦ *Dragon Naturally Speaking* (Nuance.com) is speech recognition software, which is a way to capture a first draft for those who either think better by talking or who can't take the time to write something out. "It helps me write twice as fast and the writing is better because the tone is more conversational," Paul Gillin told me.

♦ *Rev* (rev.com) is a crowdsourced transcription and translation service.

♦ *Speechpad* (speechpad.com) is a transcription and dictation service.

♦ *Speakwrite* (speakwrite.com) is similar to Speechpad.

♦ *CastingWords* (castingwords.com) is similar to Speechpad and Speakwrite.

Blog Idea Generators

These aren't writing tools per se, but they can help spark some writing ideas based on topics you want to write about.

♦ *Portent's Content Idea Generator* (portent.com/tools/title-maker) lets you enter a topic, and the idea generator spits back a bunch of content idea headlines. For example, the subject *eyeglasses* delivers "14 Ways to Be the McGyver of Eyeglasses" and "13 Secrets about Eyeglasses the Government Is Hiding." It's a fun (and often silly) way to brainstorm topics and approaches. Use it less as a prescription and more as a creative nudge.

♦ *Blog About* (impactbnd.com/blog-title-generator/blogabout) is an idea generator that's ideal when you know your topic so well that you're having a hard time coming up with a fresh or unique angle. It's more nuanced than Portent's idea generator in that it suggests several points of view (the customer experience, opinions, growth, and so on) before it gets into the nitty-gritty of specific ideas. I also like the way you can doodle right within the tools to visualize your thoughts and download a list of saved titles. (By Impact Branding & Design.)

♦ *UberSuggest* (ubersuggest.org) is technically a keyword sugges-tion tool, but it moonlights as a solid idea generator for new blog posts. Enter a word or phrase and the tool delivers a list of results containing the word or phrase, followed by related phrases that can help ignite new ideas.

♦ *Topsy* (topsy.com) is a social analytics company that allows you to search for links, tweets, photos, videos, and influencers relevant to your topic. It's useful to take a stroll through it if seeing what others are talking about helps you. Think of it as eavesdropping on the Internet.

♦ *TweakYourBiz Title Generator* (tweakyourbiz.com/tools/title-generator) delivers a comprehensive list of approaches in various categories—lists, how-to, secrets, snark, and the kitchen sink—when you enter a noun or verb. The headlines that are suggested are a little perfunctory ("The Seven Best Things About Eye-glasses"), but the title generator can help spark some new content approaches.

Google Authorship

People who write for the Web have a special way to digitally sign their work. It's called Google Authorship. It allows Google to make the connection between the writer and the content they've written. When Google makes that connection, it prominently features the author's name next to the search listing when the page appears in Google search results. (Google used to feature the author's photo as well, but it announced plans to do away with author photos in June 2014.)

Although Google Authorship may not improve the rank of a page, it can increase traffic simply by making the search listing more promi-nent. And it's not hard to set up. There are two links involved: (1) a link from the written page to the author's Google+ profile page, and (2) a link from the author's Google+ profile page to the blog or website. The first link must include a special tag, rel="author." The second link must appear in the Contributor To section of the author's About page on G+. That's it!

The writers who reap the greatest rewards from Google Authorship are the ones who follow SEO basics—keyword research and keyword usage—but it can work for anyone, even if you don't pay attention to keywords and even if you're not active on Google+. It's certainly a small thrill the first time you see your name noted in search results!

For more information, see https://plus.google.com or Andy Crestodina's piece on the MarketingProfs site: marketingprofs.com/google-authorship.

Image Sources (Or, Stock That Doesn't Stink)

The problem with stock photos is that they often look like stock photos. In other words, they're often not all that unique. So where do you find stock photos that *don't* stink and are *free or almost free*? Here are some sources for quality images that are cleared for use on any content you create—on your site, blog posts, in social media, and so on.

SEARCHABLE PHOTO DATABASES

♦ *Creative Commons* (http://search.creativecommons.org) is a nonprofit organization that enables the sharing and use of creativity and knowledge through free (and legal!) tools.

There are various types of Creative Commons licenses that range from the broad (allowing any type of use with no attribution) to the more restrictive (allowing only certain uses in certain situations). The Search function is like the Costco of stock photos: it allows you to widely search a bunch of different free sources from the same place, including some of the top sources for nonstockish stock photos like Flickr, Google Images, and Pixabay—all popular sources in their own right.

♦ *Compfight* (compfight.com) says it "helps you locate images you actually want to find." It's not affiliated with or owned by Flickr, but it's a handy way to find Flickr images specific to your licensing needs.

- *Dreamstime* (dreamstime.com) has free images that are frequently updated.
- *PhotoPin* (photopin.com).
- *Free Images* (freeimages.com).
- *MorgueFile* (morguefile.com) has unique images that are free with credit to the photographer.
- *Public Domain Pictures* (publicdomainpictures.net) is a repository for images that are in the public domain (i.e., free).
- *Fotolia* (fotolia.com).
- *Ancestry Images* (ancestryimages.com) has more than 27,800 images of old and antique prints, maps, and portraits. There are some restrictions on commercial use, but the collection is unique.

Photo Collections

These collections are mostly nonsearchable (or difficult to search), but many have gorgeous photos that are a cut above what you'll find elsewhere.

- *Death to the Stock Photo* (join.deathtothestockphoto.com) gets a nod for the fun name, but it also has a high-quality collection of free images.
- *Superfamous* (superfamous.com) is free but its photos require attribution.
- *Little Visuals* (littlevisuals.co).
- *New Old Stock* (nos.twnsnd.co) offers a collection of vintage photos, free of copyright restrictions.
- *Unsplash* (unsplash.com) delivers 10 free photos every 10 days.
- *PicJumbo* (picjumbo.com).

Roll Your Own

- *Your own images*: I use a lot of my own Instagram images on my site at AnnHandley.com and (typically) in presentations and other content I produce. I often photograph oddball, random things just because I have a hunch I might be able to use it down the road in a post. Others rely on their own images as well, including Steve Garfield, Chris Penn, Lee Odden, Jesper Outzen, and my *Content Rules* coauthor C. C. Chapman.

- *Canva* (canva.com) allows you to create gorgeous graphics and images to accompany any content. I particularly like the simple, intuitive interface that puts magic wands into the hands of design muggles.
- *TinEye* (tineye.com) is a reverse image search engine. Upload an image and it can identify its source and how it's being used and modified. It's handy to identify an original photographer or source, but also handy if you're looking for a higher-resolution version of an image you want to use.

Epilogue

A writer who waits for ideal conditions under which to work will die without putting a word on paper.

—E. B. White

Done is better than perfect.

Acknowledgments for Tools

Thank you to the following for suggesting tools:

Tinu Abayomi-Paul
Carmen S. Asteinza
Jay Baer
Alan Belniak
Connie Bensen
Tristan Bishop
Margot Bloomstein
Bernie Borges
Te-ge Watts Bramhall
David Brazael
Michael Brenner
Charles Brown
Carrie Bugbee
Bobbie Carlton
Doriano Paisano Carta
Brian Carter
Christine Cavalier
Adam Cohen
Dave Cutler
Jeff Cutler
Sean D'Souza
Melanie Deardorff
Gini Dietrich
Sondra Santos Drahos
Leigh Durst
Michael Durwin
Jonas Ellison
Elaine Cohen Fogel
Jill M. Foster
Lisa Gerber

Paul Gillin
Linda Sherman Gordon
Kerry O'Shea Gorgone
Gavin Heaton
Clay Hebert
Katie Higingbotham
Carmen Hill
Whitney Hoffman
Shel Holtz
Christina Inge
Mana Ionescu
Mitch Joel
Martin Jones
Jennifer Kane
Beth Kanter
Jason Keath
Maile Keone
Doug Kessler
Arnie Kuenn
Geoff Livingston
Patricia Maranga-Redsicker
Clare McDermott
Rachel Happe McEnroe
Sean McGinnis
Steve McNamara
Alycia de Mesa
Jason Miller
Sharon Mostyn
Amber Naslund
Lisa Nirell

Jesse Noyes

Lee Odden

Maria Pergolino

Marc A. Pitman

Jane Quigley

Ross Quintana

Jo Roberts

Helen Klein Ross

Mark Schaefer

Angie Schottmuller

Kathy Lynne Sharpe

Jeff Shuey

Sonia Simone

Matt Snodgrass

Shane Snow

Jason Sohigian

Jim Storer

David B Thomas

Maria Thurrell

Meg Tripp

Vicki VanValkenburgh

Lauren Vargas

Amy Vernon

Kelly Hungerford de Vooght

John J. Wall

Frank Watson

Debbie Weil

Nick Westergaard

Paul Williams

Travis Wright

Faris Yacob

Notes

Introduction

1. Lauren Yapalater, "13 Potatoes That Look Like Channing Tatum," BuzzFeed, October 24, 2013, www.buzzfeed.com/lyapalater/potatoes-that-look-like-channing-tatum.

2. Beth Dunn, "How to Be a Writing God," YouTube video, Inbound Bold Talks (Inbound 2013 conference), January 8, 2014, www.youtube.com/watch?v=S8Q3vnPM6kk.

3. Janet Choi, "The Simplest Way to Know What Everyone's Doing at Work," Fast Company, November 21, 2013, www.fastcompany.com/3021980/dialed/the-simplest-way-to-know-what-everyones-doing-at-work.

4. Jeff Bezos, interview by Charlie Rose, Charlie Rose, PBS, aired November 15, 2012, www.charlierose.com/watch/60148245.

5. Steven Pinker, "Writing As Psychology," Exposé (Essays from the Expository Writing Program at Harvard College), 2006–2007, www.jhcwp.com/wp-content/uploads/2013/09/Expose06_07.pdf.

6. "B2B Content Marketing 2014: Benchmarks, Budgets, and Trends, North America," slide presentation, Content Marketing Institute/MarketingProfs, October 1, 2013, www.slideshare.net/mprofs/b2b-content-marketing-2014-benchmarks-budgets-and-trendsnorth-america.

Part I Writing Rules: How to Write Better (and How to Hate Writing Less)

1. Ta-Nehisi Coates, "Notes from the First Year: Some Thoughts on Teaching at MIT," Atlantic, June 11, 2013, www.theatlantic.com/national/archive/2013/06/notes-from-the-first-year-some-thoughts-on-teaching-at-mit/276743.

2. Matt Waite, "Matt Waite: How I Faced My Fears and Learned to Be Good at Math," Neiman Journalism Lab, November 13, 2013, www.niemanlab.org/2013/11/matt-waite-how-i-faced-my-fears-and-learned-to-be-good-at-math.

2 Writing Is a Habit, Not an Art

1. "Taylor Mali Answers the Question, 'Where Is Your Favorite Place to Write?'" YouTube video, posted by Taylor Mali, September 15, 2007, www.youtube.com/watch?v=O_POEIhEXRI.

2. Mason Currey, *Daily Rituals: How Artists Work* (New York: Knopf Doubleday, 2013).

3. Gretchen Rubin, "The Habits We Most Want to Foster," *Psychology Today* 21 (February 2014), www.psychologytoday.com/blog/the-happiness-project/201402/the-habits-we-most-want-foster-or-the-essential-seven.

4. INBOUND Bold Talks: Beth Dunn "How To Be a Writing God," YouTube video, posted by HubSpot, 8 January 2014, www.youtube.com/watch?v=S8Q3vnPM6kk.

5. Jeff Goins, "Why You Need to Write Every Day," *Goins, Writer* (blog), www.goinswriter.com/write-every-day.

3 Shed High School Rules

1. Todd Balf, "The Story Behind the SAT Overhaul," *New York Times Magazine*, March 6, 2014, www.nytimes.com/2014/03/09/magazine/the-story-behind-the-sat-overhaul.html and "Revising the SAT," WBUR, March 6, 2014, radioboston.wbur.org/2014/03/06/sat-changes.

5 Place the Most Important Words (and Ideas) at the Beginning of Each Sentence

1. "Simply Put: A Guide for Creating Easy-to-Understand Materials, Third Edition," Centers for Disease Control and Prevention, July 2010, www.cdc.gov/healthliteracy/pdf/simply_put.pdf.

6 Follow a Writing GPS

1. Chip Scanlan, "Ten Paradoxes of the Writing Life," Poynter, August 2, 2002, www.poynter.org/uncategorized/1576/ten-paradoxes-of-the-writing-life.

7 The More the Think, the Easier the Ink

1. Robert Mankoff, "Inking and Thinking," *New Yorker* blog, June 16, 2010, www.newyorker.com/online/blogs/cartoonists/2010/06/inking-and-thinking.html.

9 Embrace The Ugly First Draft

1. Thomas Newkirk and Lisa C. Miller, eds., *The Essential Don Murray: Lessons from America's Greatest Writing Teacher* (Portsmouth, NH: Boynton-Cook Publishers, 2009).

10 Swap Places with Your Reader

1. Thomas Newkirk and Lisa C. Miller, eds., *The Essential Don Murray: Lessons from America's Greatest Writing Teacher* (Portsmouth, NH: Boynton-Cook Publishers, 2009).

2. *The Economist Style Guide*, accessed June 6, 2014, www.economist.com/style-guide/introduction.

12   Develop Pathological Empathy

1. www.siriusdecisions.com/Who-We-Are.aspx.

14   Start with *Dear Mom* . . .

1. Chip Scanlon, "Being Blocked Is Part of the Process," Poynter, March 2, 2011, www.poynter.org/how-tos/newsgathering-storytelling/chip-on-your-shoulder/21037/being-blocked-is-part-of-the-process/.
2. Colin Nissan, "The Ultimate Guide to Writing Better Than You Normally Do," Timothy McSweeney's Internet Tendency (McSweeneys.net), April 10, 2012, www.mcsweeneys.net/articles/the-ultimate-guide-to-writing-better-than-you-normally-do.
3. John McPhee, "Draft No. 4," *New Yorker*, April 29, 2013.

15   If You Take a Running Start, Cover Your Tracks

1. Jim Newell, "How to Win Memorial Day: A Holiday Guide to Arguing with Right-Wing Relatives," Salon, May 26, 2014, www.salon.com/2014/05/26/how_to_win_memorial_day_a_holiday_guide_to_arguing_with_right_wing_relatives.

17   'A Good Lede Invites You to the Party and a Good Kicker Makes You Wish You Could Stay Longer'

1. Here's some content trivia. The print publishing industry made up *lede* to replace *lead*. It was done to avoid confusion in a publishing world that used lead (the metal) to set type by hand, and in which *lead* referred to the amount of spacing between the baselines of text—as measured in strips of lead inserted between lines of type (text). These days, *lede* and *lead*, when used to refer to the opening of a story, are interchangeable.
2. Matthew Stibbe, "Want to Write Well? Open with a Punch, Close with a Kick," *Bad Language* (blog), accessed June 9, 2014, www.badlanguage.net/want-to-write-well-open-with-a-punch-close-with-a-kick.
3. Ernest Nicastro, "Seven Score and Seven Years Ago: Writing Lessons We Can Learn from Lincoln's Masterpiece," MarketingProfs, April 27, 2010, www.marketingprofs.com/articles/2010/3568/seven-score-and-seven-years-ago-writing-lessons-we-can-learn-from-lincolns-masterpiece.

4. "101 Places to Get F*cked Up Before You Die," Thrillist, December 30, 2013, www .thrillist.com/travel/nation/excerpts-from-101-places-to-get-f-cked-up-before-you-die-thrillist-nation.

5. Demian Farnworth, "13 Damn Good Ideas from 13 Dead Copywriters," *Copyblogger* (blog), accessed June 9, 2014, www.copyblogger.com/ideas-from-dead-copywriters.

6. Franchesca Ramsey, "This School Struggled with Detentions, so They Asked for Students' Help. Guess What? It's Working," Upworthy, accessed June 9, 2014, www.upworthy.com/this-school-struggled-with-detentions-so-they-asked-for-students-help-guess-what-its-working.

7. Leah Hunter, "Are Wearables Over?," *Fast Company*, accessed June 9, 2014, www .fastcompany.com/3028879/most-innovative-companies/are-wearables-over.

8. Richard Brody, "The Secrets of Godzilla," *New Yorker* blog, April 18, 2014, www .newyorker.com/online/blogs/movies/2014/04/the-secrets-of-godzilla.html.

9. "Honey Maid Takes on Haters, and Now I Want Graham Crackers," www .annhandley.com/2014/04/04/honey-maid-takes-haters-now-want-graham-crackers/.

10. Matthew Stibbe, "Want to Write Well? Open with a Punch, Close with a Kick," Bad Language, http://www.badlanguage.net/want-to-write-well-open-with-a-punch-close-with-a-kick.

11. "How to Use Instagram in a Genius Way," AnnHandley.com.

18 Show, Don't Tell

1. Aaron Orendorff, "Getting Your Customers to Hold It, Love It, Give It Money," IconiContent, March 3, 2014, iconicontent.com/blog/getting-your-customers-to-hold-it-love-it-and-give-it-money.

2. Natalie Goldberg, *Writing Down the Bones* (Boston: Shambhala, 1986).

19 Use Familiar Yet Surprising Analogies

1. "NSA Files Decoded," *The Guardian*, November 1, 2013, www.theguardian.com/world/interactive/2013/nov/01/snowden-nsa-files-surveillance-revelations-decoded.

20 Approach Writing Like Teaching

1. Anne Lamott, *Bird by Bird* (Anchor Books, 1995).

21 Keep It Simple—but Not Simplistic

1. Georgy Cohen, "How Not to Make a Website," January 23, 2013, Crosstown Digital Communications blog, takethecrosstown.com/2013/01/23/how-not-to-make-a-website.

25   Be Rabid about Readability

1. "Test Your Document's Readability," Microsoft Support, accessed June 9, 2014, http://office.microsoft.com/en-us/word-help/test-your-document-s-readability-HP010354286.aspx?CTT=1#_Toc342546555.

29   Use Real Words

1. William Struck Jr. and E. B. White, *The Elements of Style*, 4th ed. (Longman, 1999; original published 1920).

34   Ditch Adverbs, Except When They Adjust the Meaning

1. Stephen King, *On Writing: A Memoir of the Craft* (New York: Scribner, 2000).

35   Use Clichés Only Once in a Blue Moon

1. Nigel Fountain, *Clichés: Avoid Them Like the Plague* (London: Michael O'Mara Books, 2011).

37   Break Some Grammar Rules (At Least These Five)

1. Mignon Fogarty, "Split Infinitives," QuickAndDirtyTips.com, August 20, 2010, www.quickanddirtytips.com/education/grammar/split-infinitives.
2. Mignon Fogarty, "Ending a Sentence with a Preposition." QuickAndDirtyTips.com, March 31, 2011, www.quickanddirtytips.com/education/grammar/ending-a-sentence-with-a-preposition.

38   Learn Words You're Probably Misusing or Confusing with Other Words

1. Jatin Anand, "Woman Goes Missing; Disinterested Police 'Guess' She Eloped, Shut Case," *Hindustan Times*, March 10, 2014, www.hindustantimes.com/india-news/newdelhi/woman-goes-missing-disinterested-police-guess-she-eloped-shut-case/article1-1193388.aspx.
2. Jack Torrance, "Eight in Ten SMEs Disinterested in Seeking Finance," February 27, 2014, Real Business newsletter, http://realbusiness.co.uk/article/25766-eight-in-ten-smes-disinterested-in-seeking-finance-.
3. Doug Padilla, "Soaring Noah Reluctant to Accept Praise," ESPN blog, accessed June 10, 2014, http://espn.go.com/blog/chicago/bulls/post/_/id/18260/soaring-noah-reluctant-to-accept-praise.
4. Maxwell Strachan, "Two Charts That Will Enrage Everyone (Well, Except Bankers)," *Huffington Post*, March 13, 2014, www.huffingtonpost.com/2014/03/12/wall-street-minimum-wage_n_4951843.html.

5. Tom Porter, "Silk Road 2.0 Was Hub for Illicit Trade in . . . Tesco Vouchers," International Business Times, March 9, 2014, www.ibtimes.co.uk/silk-road-2-0-was-hub-illicit-trade-tesco-vouchers-1439530.

6. Via @HonestToddler on Twitter, July 8, 2013, twitter.com/HonestToddler/status/354267183938945025.

7. Bunmi Laditan, "How to Put a Toddler to Bed in 100 Easy Steps," *Honest Toddler* (blog), March 14, 2014, www.thehonesttoddler.com/2014/03/how-to-put-toddler-to-bed-in-100-easy.html.

8. Austin Kleon, *Show Your Work: 10 Ways to Share Your Creativity and Get Discovered* (New York: Workman Publishing, 2014).

39 Scuse Me While I Kiss This Guy

1. "Mondegreen vs. Eggcorn," The Word Detective, August 24, 2009, www.word-detective.com/2009/08/mondegreen-vs-eggcorn.

41 Tell How You'll Change the World

1. Anne Lamott, *Bird by Bird: Some Instructions on Writing and Life* (New York: Anchor, 1995).

2. "The Scarecrow," Chipotle video, September 11, 2013, www.youtube.com/watch?v=lUtnas5ScSE; Matthew Yglesias, "You Want to Watch Chipotle's Amazing 'Scarecrow' Video," Slate, September 12, 2013, www.slate.com/blogs/moneybox/2013/09/12/chipotle_scarecrow_video_is_totally_amazing.html; Schuyter Velasco, "Chipotle Ad Campaign Takes on 'Big Food,' Targets Millennials," *Christian Science Monitor* online, September 13, 2013, www.csmonitor.com/Business/2013/0913/Chipotle-ad-campaign-takes-on-Big-Food-targets-Millennials-video; Eliza Barclay, "Taking Down Big Food Is the Name of Chipotle's New Game," National Public Radio blog, September 12, 2013, www.npr.org/blogs/thesalt/2013/09/12/221736558/taking-down-big-food-is-the-name-of-chipotles-new-game.

42 Tell the Story Only You Can Tell

1. Neil Gaiman, interview by Chris Hardwick, podcast #106, Nerdist, July 12, 2011, www.nerdist.com/pepisode/nerdist-podcast-106-neil-gaiman.

43 Voice and Tone

1. Victor Doyno, *Writing Huck Finn: Mark Twain's Creative Process* (Philadelphia: University of Pennsylvania Press, 1992).

44 Look to Analogy instead of Example

1. Mason Cooley. (n.d.). Brainyquote.com. Retrieved June 29, 2014, www.brainyquote.com/quotes/quotes/m/masoncoole395060.html.

2. Seth Godin, "Analogies, Metaphors, and Your Problem," August 8, 2012, http:// sethgodin.typepad.com/seths_blog/2012/08/analogies-metaphors-and-your-problem.html.

3. Jess Bidgood, "Father and Son Declare a Political Truce, for 60 Seconds," *New York Times* online, September 17, 2013, http://thecaucus.blogs.nytimes.com/2013/09/ 17/father-and-son-declare-a-political-truce-for-60-seconds/?_php=true&_type= blogs&_php=true&_type=blogs&_r=1&; Ben Jacobs, "Inside Carl Sciortino's Viral Campaign Ad," *Daily Beast*, September 19, 2013, www.thedailybeast.com/ articles/2013/09/19/inside-carl-sciortino-s-viral-campaign-ad.html; Carl Sciortino Sr. and Carl Sciortino Jr., interview by Chris Matthews, *Hardball*, September 19, 2013, www.msnbc.com/msnbc/tea-party-dads-son-comes-out-liberal; Aaron Blake, "House Candidate Comes Out to Father . . . as a Liberal," Washington Post online, September 17, 2013, www.washingtonpost.com/blogs/post-politics/ wp/2013/09/17/house-candidate-comes-out-to-father-as-a-liberal.

Part IV   Publishing Rules

1. Shane Snow, "Contently's Code of Ethics for Journalism and Content Marketing," Contently, 1 August 1, 2012, http://contently.com/strategist/2012/08/01/ethics.

45   Wait. What's Brand Journalism?

1. Dan Lyons, "The CMO's Guide to Brand Journalism," PDF from Hubspot, http:// www.hubspot.com/cmos-guide-to-brand-journalism.

47   See Content Moments Everywhere

1. Laura Mazzuca Toops, "4 Ways Insurance Might Respond if Godzilla Attacks," Property Casualty 360, May 22, 2014, www.propertycasualty360.com/2014/05/22/ 4-ways-insurance-might-respond-if-godzilla-attacks.

48   Post News That's Really News

1. Donald M. Murray, *Writing to Deadline: The Journalist at Work* (Portsmouth, NH: Heinemann, 2000).

51   Fact-Check

1. Matt Savener, "Why We Fact-Check Every Post on Upworthy," Upworthy, February 24, 2014, blog.upworthy.com/post/77713114830/why-we-fact-check-every-post-on-upworthy.

52   Approach Content with 'Mind Like Water'

1. Tom Bentley, "Mark Twain's 10-Sentence Course on Branding and Marketing," MarketingProfs, July 15, 2013, www.marketingprofs.com/articles/2013/11152/mark-twains-10-sentence-course-on-branding-and-marketing.

2. Jason A. Miller, "5 Rock n Roll Quotes to Inspire Content Marketing Greatness," LinkedIn, February 11, 2014, www.linkedin.com/today/post/article/201402110-75824-19647510-5-rock-n-roll-quotes-to-inspire-content-marketing-greatness.

55   Cite as You Write

1. See http://en.wikipedia.org/wiki/Wikipedia:Academic_use.

56   Curate Ethically

1. Maria Popova, "What We Talk About When We Talk About Curation," Brainpickings, March 16, 2012, www.brainpickings.org/index.php/2012/03/16/percolate-curation/.

2. Curata, "2014 Content Marketing Tactics Planner," Curata, info.curata.com/rs/hivefire/images/Curata_ContentMarketingTacticsPlanner2014.pdf.

3. Pawan Deshpande, "10 Steps to Ethical Content Curation," MarketingProfs, December 9, 2013, www.marketingprofs.com/articles/2013/12242/10-steps-to-ethical-content-curation.

61   Writing for Twitter

1. Richard Lea, "Penguin Cookbook Calls for 'Freshly Ground Black People'," *The Guardian*, April 19, 2010, www.theguardian.com/books/2010/apr/19/penguin-cook-book.

62   Writing with Hashtags

1. "'#Hashtag' with Jimmy Fallon and Justin Timberlake," *Tonight Show Starring Jimmy Fallon*, YouTube video, September 24, 2013, www.youtube.com/watch?v=57dzaMaouXA#t=20.

2. Nick Ehrenberg, "The Hashtag Test: Best and Worst Practices for Social Media Marketers," *Top Rank Marketing* (blog), April 8, 2014, www.toprankblog.com/2014/04/hashtag-marketing.

3. Susan Orlean, "Hash," *New Yorker* online, June 29, 2010, www.newyorker.com/online/blogs/susanorlean/2010/06/hash.html.

64 Writing for Facebook

1. "Adobe Digital Index: The Social Intelligence Report," Q1 2014, www.cmo.com/content/dam/CMO_Other/ADI/SocialIntelligence_Q12014/Q1_2014_social_intelligence_report.pdf.

66 Writing Your LinkedIn Profile

1. Deep Nishar, "The Next Three Billion," LinkedIn blog, April 18, 2014, blog.linkedin.com/2014/04/18/the-next-three-billion/.
2. "Being Responsible Is Overrated," LinkedIn (press release), December 10, 2013, press.linkedin.com/News-Releases/324/Being-Responsible-is-Overrated.
3. Tobias Schremmer, "Don't Be This Person on LinkedIn: Headline Don'ts and Do's," MarketingProfs, May 28, 2014, www.marketingprofs.com/opinions/2014/25214/dont-be-this-person-on-linkedin-headline-donts-and-dos.

67 Writing for Email

1. Carolyn Nye, "Email Marketing in 2014: How to Avoid Spam Folders," Practical-Ecommerce, March 24, 2014, www.practicalecommerce.com/articles/65858-Email-Marketing-in-2014-How-to-Avoid-Spam-Folders.
2. Ayaz Nanji, "4Q13 Email Trends and Benchmarks," MarketingProfs, February 18, 2014, www.marketingprofs.com/charts/2014/24405/4q13-e-mail-trends-and-benchmarks.
3. Authority Intensive event, speaker Joanna Wiebe, my.copyblogger.com/authority-intensive/.

69 Writing Headlines

1. Farhad Manjo, "BuzzFeed's Brazen, Nutty Growth Plan," *Wall Street Journal* online, October 14, 2013, http://online.wsj.com/news/articles/SB10001424052702304500404579129590411867328; Jeff Bercovici, "With 30M Uniques under Its Belt, Upworthy Is Ready to Monetize," *Forbes* online, July 1, 2013, www.forbes.com/sites/jeffbercovici/2013/07/01/with-30m-uniques-under-its-belt-upworthy-is-ready-to-monetize.
2. Brian Carey, "What BuzzFeed Can Teach You about Writing a Viral-Worthy Headline," *Intuit Small Business* (blog), September 17, 2013, http://blog.intuit.com/marketing/what-buzzfeed-can-teach-you-about-writing-a-viral-worthy-headline.
3. David B. Thomas, "I Didn't Believe This Amazing Thing About Content Marketing Until I Realized I Was Using Ketchup Wrong," *Salesforce* (blog), May 16, 2014, http://blogs.salesforce.com/company/2014/05/content-marketing-trend.html.

4. Peter Koechley, "Why the Title Matters More Than the Talk," *Upworthy Insider* (blog), May, 19, 2014, blog.upworthy.com/post/26345634089/why-the-title-matters-more-than-the-talk.

72   Writing Infographics That Won't Make People Mock Infographics

1. "Top 13 Infographics That Mock Infographics," *SaveDelete* (blog), April 5, 2012, http://savedelete.com/2012/04/05/top-13-infographics-that-mock-infographics/25174?q=/top-13-infographics-that-mock-infographics.html#.

2. "How Big Will Cloud Computing Be in 2015? Consider the Cupcake," YouTube video, Cisco, www.youtube.com/watch?v=D34G30lWgg8.

73   Writing Better Blog Posts

1. Ayaz Nanji, "Blog Best-Practices and Benchmarks," MarketingProfs, April 28, 2014, www.marketingprofs.com/charts/2014/25006/blog-best-practices-and-benchmarks.

74   Writing Annual Reports (or Annual Wrap-Ups)

1. Hubspotting (2013 Annual Report), *HubSpot*, http://hubspot.uberflip.com/i/249529.

2. 2013 Annual Report, Warby Parker, www.warbyparker.com/annual-report-2013.

3. Ann-Christine Diaz, "Warby Parker Unveils 2013 Annual Report—and It's 365 Days Long," *AdAge*, January 10, 2014, adage.com/article/news/warby-parker-unveils-365-day-2013-annual-report/291006.

4. 2013 Annual Report (microsite), MailChimp, http://mailchimp.com/2013/#by-the-numbers.

5. 2012 Annual Report, Calgary Zoo, April 2013, http://instagram.com/calgaryzoo2012ar.

6. Leo Widrich, "From 0 to 1,000,000 Users: The Journey and Statistics of Buffer," September 19, 2013, http://blog.bufferapp.com/from-0-to-1000000-users-the-journey-and-statistics-of-buffer.

Part VI   Content Tools

1. Steve Brocklehurst, "Why Are Fountain Pen Sales Rising," *BBC News Magazine*, May 22, 2012, www.bbc.com/news/magazine-18071830.

2. Lito Apostolakou, "Jane Austen, Her Pen, Her Ink," December 8, 2010, http://writinginstruments.blogspot.co.uk/2010/12/jane-austen-her-pen-her-ink.html?q=jane+austen.

Index